Vikings in Wales

An Archaeological Quest

by Mark Redknap

NATIONAL MUSEUMS & GALLERIES OF WALES
CARDIFF 2000

For Catrin, Caio & Ianto

© First published in 2000 by
National Museums & Galleries of Wales
Cathays Park
Cardiff
CF10 3NP

Also published in Welsh as *Y Llychlynwyr yng Nhgymru.
Ymchwil Archaeolegol* (2000)

ISBN 0 7200 0486 1

British Library Cataloguing in Publication Data
A CIP catalogue record for this book is available from the
British Library.

Typeset and designed by Arwel Hughes, National Museums
& Galleries of Wales.

Printed in Wales by MWL Print Group Ltd, Pontypool.

Contents

Introduction

In the past, few publications covering the history and archaeology of the Vikings have featured evidence from Wales, even though the familiar names of Anglesey, Fishguard, Skomer and Caldey are part of our 'Scandinavian' heritage in the modern landscape. This book aims to provide an overview of their impact, through summaries of historical evidence and the results of recent archaeological excavations, and by means of drawings, plans and photographs of some of the actual artefacts and sites of the period. Where appropriate, these are placed within the wider context of what was happening during this period elsewhere in Britain and in Ireland. In many respects, our knowledge of Viking Age Wales is as yet incomplete and at times hypothesis is presented here to await the test of future investigation.

Piecing together the full story is a process of detection. Some advances stem from routine work and contact with the public, such as the voluntary reporting of archaeological finds. For example, in 1992 a package of objects from a site on Anglesey arrived at the Department of Archaeology & Numismatics for identification. The parcel contained some coins and three small lead weights, which were dated to the eighth, ninth and tenth centuries AD. The merchants' weights were particularly interesting, hinting at significant Scandinavian activity in the vicinity of the find-spot.

Not long afterwards, I found myself following a narrow, tree-shaded lane to the site which meandered as it negotiated the dips between limestone ridges to an old stone-grey farmhouse. Welcomed by Roger Tebbutt, the farmer, we trudged across the fields to inspect the various find-spots and then retired to the farmhouse to share our thoughts.

A battered biscuit tin was placed on the table and I was invited to examine an assortment of bits and pieces collected from the fields over the years. There, at the very bottom, lay a short rod with a green-coloured patina - the upper half of a copper alloy pin of tenth-century type, well-known from excavations at locations such as Viking Dublin. Was it found close to the coins or weights? What sorts of activities did the finds represent? Could further pieces of this puzzle be found? So began a new phase in our quest for evidence of the Vikings in Wales.

Mark Redknap, Cardiff. May 2000

Heathen Men

The term *Víking*, first used in modern English in 1808, tends now to be applied to all Scandinavians during the period from the mid-eighth century to about the end of the eleventh century AD. During this 'Viking Age', the Old Norse (Norwegian) term *víkingr* referred to a sea-borne pirate or robber, someone who went *í víking*, or fighting and harrying at sea. Beyond Scandinavia, other terms in Latin and Welsh were used for these raiders, such as 'gentiles' *(Kenedloed)*, 'Black Gentiles' *(Kenedloed Duon* or *Llu Du)*, 'pagans' *(Paganiaid)*, 'foreigners' and 'Black Norsemen' *(Normanyeit Duon)* as used in the Welsh annals, or *Ostmen* ('men from the east'). Contemporary writers were not always certain where the raiders came from and, indeed, very often a band of Vikings would actually have been made up of people from different regions. Archaeological and historical evidence suggests that a significant number crossed from Norway to the north and west of Britain, Ireland, Iceland and some to Greenland. Danes favoured England and also crossed to Ireland, while Swedes favoured the Baltic countries. The term *Viking* is used here to denote those Scandinavian peoples in general who engaged in raiding. On occasions the term *Viking* is used to signify a period, in accordance with established practice.

While limited Scandinavian trading with Britain and Ireland took place before the raids began at the end of the eighth century, for most inhabitants the first Vikings to be encountered were pagan warrior pirates who had learnt to master the seaways. In time, settlements, trading centres and territories were established, and the later phases of activity are known by different hybrid terms: 'Hiberno-Norse' around the Irish Sea, 'Anglo-Scandinavian' in northern England, and 'Cambro-Norse' for the period *c. 850 - c.* 1100 in Wales. It is not easy to consider the last without taking into account events in its neighbouring regions.

Historical sources record a series of terrifying attacks by Viking marauders in search of portable wealth (such as slaves, captives for ransom or bullion) from the late eighth century on the coasts of Britain, France and Ireland. Some victims saw the raids as divine punishment on a sinful people (as recorded in the late eighth century by the Northumbrian churchman and scholar Alcuin, writing from Charlemagne's court). Modern research has proposed a variety of factors for this rise in piracy, though some are now questioned. These include population growth and a consequent demand for more land (expansion into marginal lands in Norway is now thought to have begun later), developments in shipbuilding, a growth in trade and the lure of rich, undefended coastal sites in western Europe. Some Viking leaders were forced into exile because of changes within Scandinavian society, such as the growing centralisation of power and wealth. Some Vikings raided in order to build up their wealth and power before attempting to regain positions at home, while others sought to establish reputations or acquire land abroad.

While the Vikings are often regarded as plunderers and conquerors, and the episodic contact with Britain was certainly violent and disruptive, there is another view. The Scandinavians were also explorers and colonisers and those who settled included merchants, farmers and skilled craftsmen. Their impact varied considerably between regions and the evidence for their presence in Wales differs greatly from that of other areas of Britain which were completely 'Scandinavianised' (such as

dec mlyneð a deugeint ac wythgant oeð oed krist pan laðawð y paganyeid gyngen.
'Eight hundred and fifty [=852] was the year of Christ when the Pagans slew Cyngen.'

1 Manuscript entry (top left) from the Chronicle of the Princes (Brut y Tywysogyon; *translation by* T. Jones) *recording the first raids on Wales. (Peniarth 20C; folio 69R. By permission of the National Library of Wales)*

Orkney and Shetland). The quest for a contemporary record of Viking contact and for signs of their relationships with the native population of Wales, involves the disciplines of history, linguistics, archaeology and numismatics. This pursuit involves disentangling popular romantic ideas and fictitious narrative from the more complex and reliable evidence of archaeological investigation.

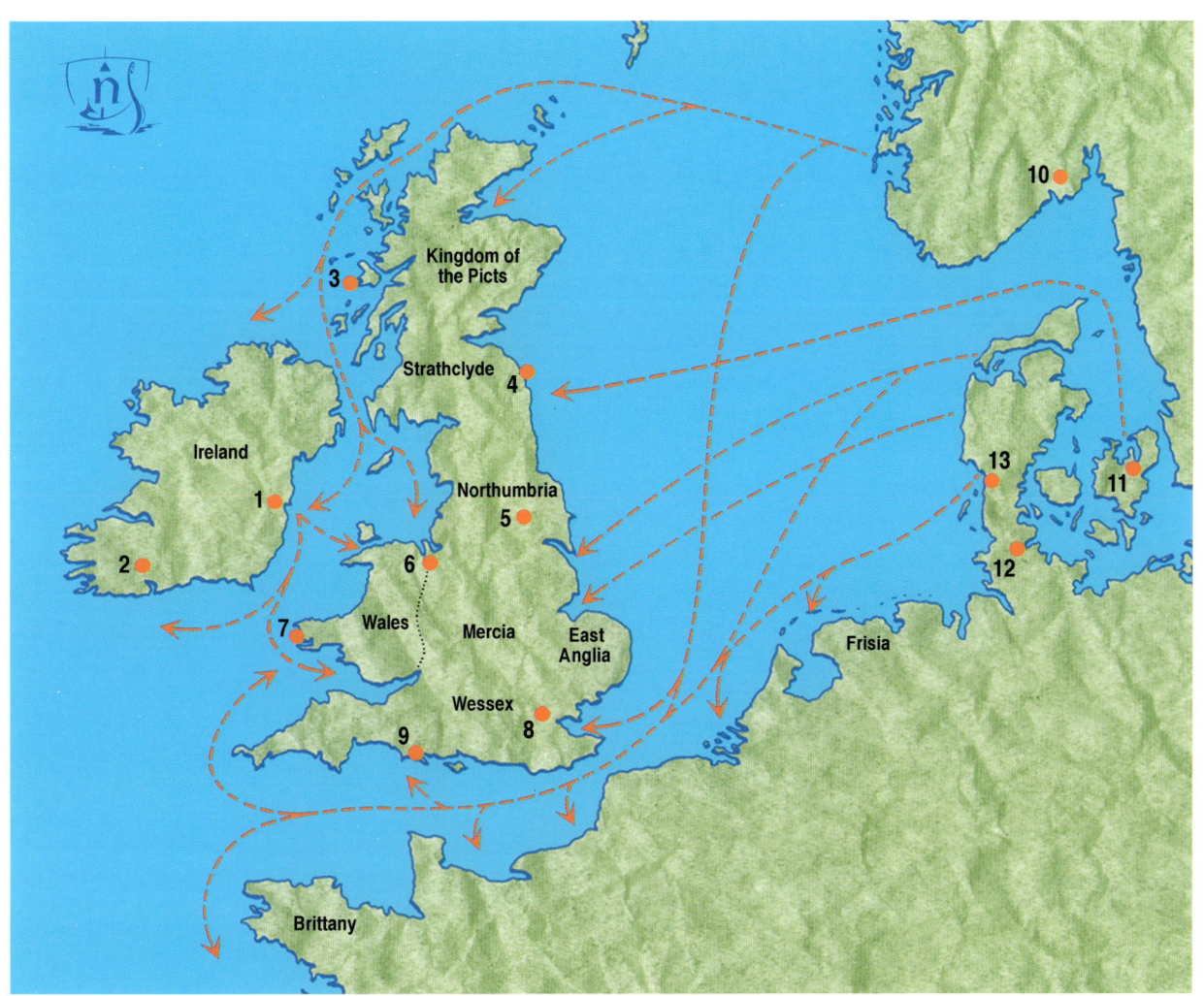

2 Main sea routes in the Viking period. 1. Dublin; 2. Cork; 3. Iona; 4. Lindisfarne; 5. York; 6. Chester; 7. St David's; 8. London; 9. Portland Bill; 10. Kaupang; 11. Roskilde; 12. Hedeby; 13. Ribe.

3 *The early medieval monastery on the island of Iona in north-west Scotland was frequently raided by Vikings (including the years 795, 802, 806, 825). According to the annals, in 878 St Columba's shrine and other relics* 'came to Ireland in flight from the foreigners'.

VIKINGS' RAIDS ON GLAMORGAN.

BISHOP OF LLANDAFF AS A HOSTAGE.

918 INVASION RE-TOLD

A BLANK PERIOD IN WELSH ARCHÆOLOGY.

Dr. R. E. Mortimer Wheeler, M.C., F.S.A., keeper of the London Museum and formerly director of the National Museum of Wales, gave a lecture before the Cardiff College Archæological Society on Friday (when Miss Mildred Johnson presided) on "The Heathen Men," which is one of the descriptions given to the Norwegian and Danish invaders of Great Britain and Ireland, who settled here between the ninth century and the Norman Conquest. Dr. Wheeler said these invaders came to Glamorgan as early as the year 795, and when they returned in the year 918 they captured the Bishop of Llandaff and held him to ransom until his freedom was secured by the payment to them by King Edward of a sum of £40, which, of course, would represent a much bigger figure in the present day. (Laughter.) Although it was known from placenames and historical evidence that these Vikings, as they were called, ...

Dr. R. E. Mortimer Wheeler, M.C., F.S.A.

THE UNIVERSITY COLLEGE OF SOUTH WALES AND MONMOUTHSHIRE ARCHAEOLOGICAL SOCIETY AND THE NATIONAL MUSEUM OF WALES

request the pleasure of the presence of you and your friends at

A LECTURE

TO BE DELIVERED AT

...IVERSITY COLLEGE, CATHAYS PARK, CARDIFF,

On Friday, the 26th November, 1926,

at 7.30 o'clock p.m. by

.... MORTIMER WHEELER, M.C., F.S.A.,

Entitled: "HEATHEN MEN."

The Welsh Annals

The annals of early Wales (*Annales Cambriae*), beside other records, form an important source of information written in Latin on events during the Cambro-Norse period. Annals were written in the monasteries as brief year-by-year accounts of events added to the church calendar of events. At St David's, where the *Annales Cambriae* were compiled, contemporary records were maintained from the late eighth to the early thirteenth centuries, using available sources to fill in earlier events. The medieval collections known as the 'Chronicle of the Princes' (*Brut y Tywysogyon*), compiled at centres such as Strata Florida in the thirteenth century, are Welsh versions of a Latin text based on the annals, and sometimes contain additional details.

4 *Report from the* **Western Mail** *in 1926 of a lecture on Viking Age Glamorgan by Mortimer Wheeler, Director of the National Museum of Wales (1924-26).*

Birth of a Viking Myth

Apart from the evidence of the annals, no Welsh chronicler produced a coherent story for the events of the ninth and tenth centuries. In a fascinating account of a tour through Wales with Archbishop Baldwin in 1188, the dynamic churchman and scholar Gerald of Wales *(Giraldus Cambrensis)* made just two comments on the Scandinavian impact besides references to the actions of 'pirates' recorded in the annals. He asserted that the Danish and Norwegian invasions had the effect of corrupting language in the northern regions of England, whereas Welsh, Cornish and Breton remained closer to original British speech (certainly the impact on the Welsh language was negligible). Secondly, he thought that traditional choral singing and part-singing in Wales was similar to that across the Humber and in Yorkshire and he credited the northern English with having taken their part-singing from the Danes and Norwegians: demonstrating an awareness of a Scandinavian past.

From the late eighteenth century, new senses of national identity led people from various parts of Europe to seek something tangible about their origins within the Christian culture they shared. The Vikings initially represented barbarian culture. In some countries, the romantic appeal of the Viking sagas soon combined with a revival of interest in the Northern World and a search for close 'northern' ancestors, primitive but noble souls. In Britain, the Vikings were in a sense re-invented in accordance with Victorian notions of race, fighting spirit and 'the benefits of Viking blood running through British veins'.

Despite the limited number of references in early literature to the Vikings in Wales (such as the tenth-century poem *Armes Prydain,* 'The Prophecy of Britain'), a level of popular interest in Norsemen and Danes was sustained here as elsewhere in Britain during the nineteenth century which reflected the climate of romanticism pervading English historical novels of the time. Interest in the Viking sagas was stimulated, and while these late texts cannot be regarded as accurate historical sources, some of the saga authors display a familiarity and awareness of certain regions, including possibly Wales, and reflect the Scandinavian view.

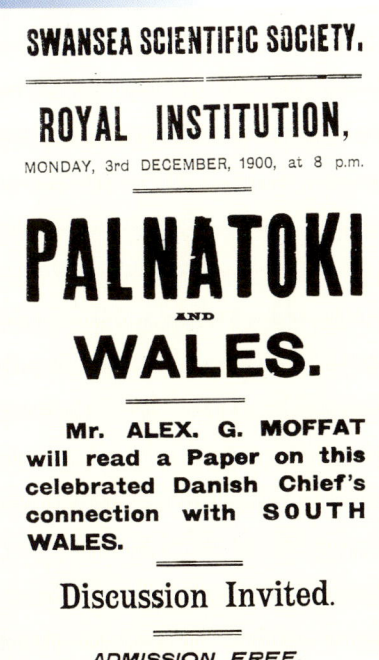

5 Advertisement for a public lecture by Moffat on the Vikings.

In the 1860s, Welshman George Ernest John Powell of Nanteos, Cardiganshire (1842-82), friend of Swinburne and Longfellow, published poems under the nom-de-plume *Miölnir Nanteos* (an allusion to the hammer *Mjöllni*, belonging to the Norse god Thór). He also collaborated with the Icelandic philologist Eiríkur Magnússon on a translation of *Hávarðar saga Ísfirðings*, Icelandic legends collected by Jón Árnasson (1864, 1866). One of the foremost writers in the 1890s, the West-Country clergyman Reverend Sabine Baring-Gould, was the author of *Grettir the Outlaw: A Story of Iceland* (1891), and collaborated with John Fisher on *Lives of the British Saints*. Narrative sources such as these 'lives' tend to concentrate on dramatic events, such as raids on churches, and are therefore often over-dramatised.

Recent historical and archaeological research has been used by authors of historical fiction. *The People of the Black Mountains* (1990), Raymond Williams' novel of dramatic episodes in the lives of the people of the Black Mountains in Breconshire, describes a fictitious attack by *Gentiles* on Llan-gors crannog, and combat between their leader 'Agnar' and the historically attested Tewdwr ap Elisedd, king of Brycheiniog, while another episode is based on the eleventh-century attack by Gruffudd ap Llywelyn, assisted by *Black Gentiles*, on Gwent and the sacking of Hereford. This book was published shortly before a campaign of excavation by the National Museums & Galleries of Wales and Cardiff University on Llan-gors crannog, which established

6 *George E.J. Powell of Nanteos, taken in 1860. (By permission of The National Library of Wales)*

that it had been built in the late ninth century, and was probably a *llys* or royal court of the ruling dynasty of Brycheiniog, during the reigns of Elisedd ap Tewdwr and Tewdwr ap Elisedd. It was probably destroyed in 916 by a Mercian army sent into Wales by Alfred's daughter, Æthelflæd.

Ellis Peters, the queen of the historical detective story, took events recorded in the Welsh annals for the year 1144 and focused on the conflict between Owain Gwynedd and his brother Cadwaladr as a basis for her story *The Summer of the Danes* (1991). In this story, Cadwaladr returns from exile with a Norse fleet from Dublin contracted for 2000 marks.

Sagas

In Old Norse, the word saga *originally meant 'what is said', but in time came to mean a prose narrative written in the twelfth century or later. Some of the sagas were detailed stories set in the past about death and honour, based loosely on characters and events of the period, while others reflected myths, gods and romances. The difficulty lies in assessing how much of these, if any, record reliable oral tradition.*

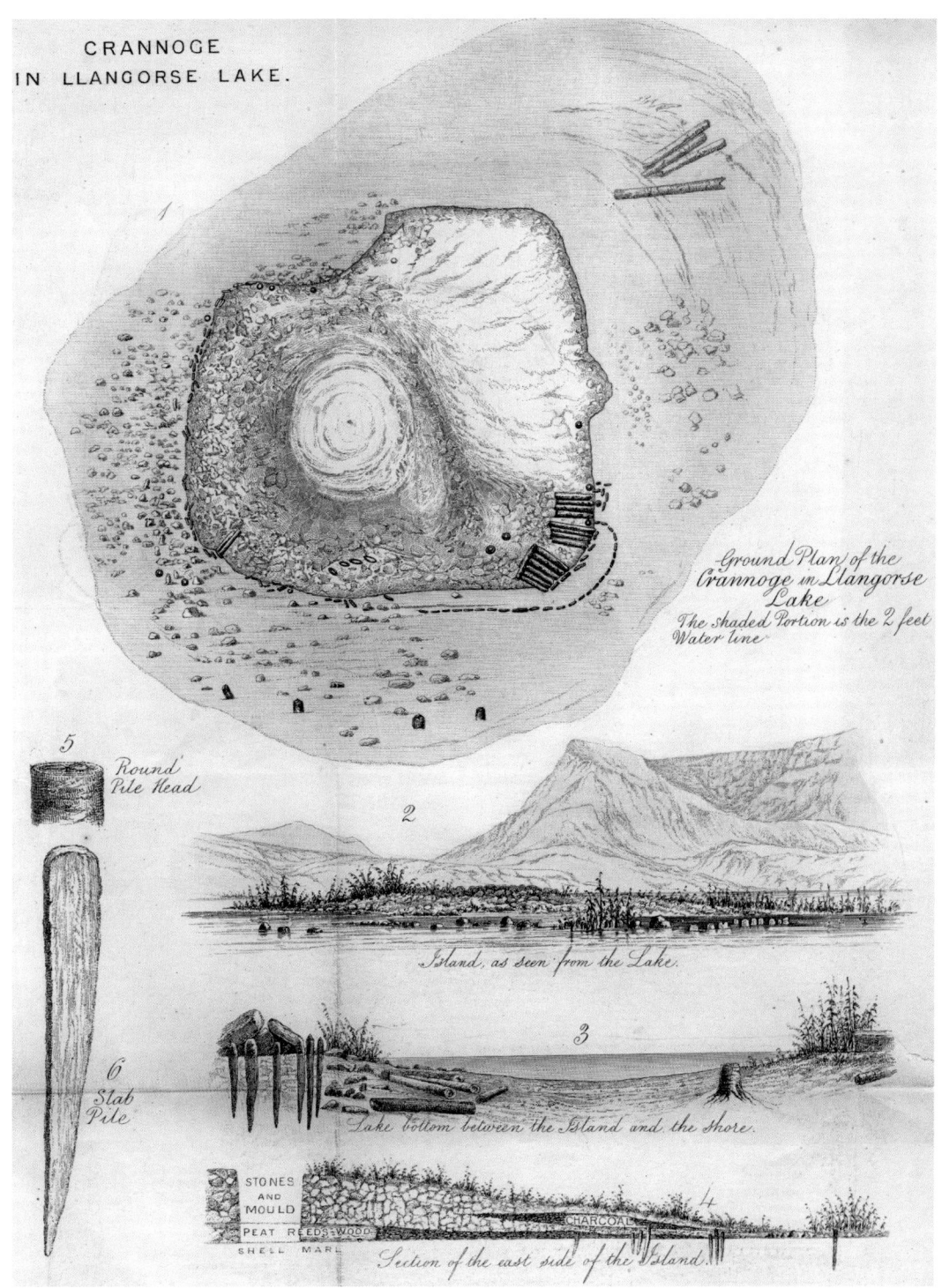

CRANNOGE
IN LLANGORSE LAKE.

1

Ground Plan of the Crannoge in Llangorse Lake
The shaded Portion is the 2 feet Water line

5
Round Pile Head

2

Island, as seen from the Lake.

6
Slab Pile

3

Lake bottom between the Island and the Shore.

STONES AND MOULD
PEAT REEDS WOOD
SHELL MARL

CHARCOAL

4

Section of the east side of the Island.

7 Plan of the royal crannog on Llan-gors Lake, Powys, published in 1870 (reproduced from Archaeologia Cambrensis*).
It is now known that the crannog was constructed between c. 890-893 or shortly thereafter, and was destroyed in 916.*

'Bretland'

The semi-legendary Icelandic *Jómsvíkinga* saga, written down around 1200, tells of a warrior community of Vikings in the Baltic. In the saga, which is set in the tenth century, the founder of 'Jómsborg' on the south coast of the Baltic, Viking leader Pálna-Tóki (foster-father of King Svein), raided *Bretland* ('Land of the British') where he married Earl Stefni's daughter Álöf and settled. Here Pálna-Tóki met Björn *hinn brezki* in Old Norse (Björn 'the Welshman'), who was put in charge of their interests. There is, however, little to suggest that the person who wrote this saga down in about the year 1200 was alluding to Wales, and Bretland here may simply represent 'a distant land about which little is known'.

Viking culture exerted a powerful hold on the nineteenth-century imagination and interest was not confined to literature, as illustrated by George Silk, who asked the Icelandic philologist Guðbrandur Vigfússon to recommend a composer 'fond of the sea' who could set his libretto on the 'spirit of Palnatoki and the Jomsborg Vikings' to music. Throughout Britain, learning was shared with the public through lectures, sometimes accompanied by lantern slides. Ship-owner and pillar of the Royal Institution at Swansea, Alexander Moffat (1855-1940) was the Glamorganshire District Secretary of the Viking Club (founded in 1892). He published an account of 'Norse place-names in Gower' and in 1900 gave an account of the 'Bretland' element of the *Jómsvíkinga saga*, attempting to show how Pálna-Tóki and Svein Forkbeard, king of Denmark and father of Cnut, settled for some time in south Wales.

8 *Romantic image by J. Finnemore from* Kormak the Viking, *a version by J.F. Hodgetts of the Icelandic* Kormák's saga, *published by The Religious Tract Society in 1902. The decorative cliché of horned or winged helmets, for which there is no archaeological evidence, persisted from the nineteenth century.*

This was an elaboration of the opinion expressed in 1848 by Swansea antiquary George Grant Francis (1814-82) to members of the British Association that 'Swansea' derived from the Old Norse *Svein's Eie* ('Sweyn's island'). Moffat had no doubt that Svein Forkbeard was the person behind the name, and that Svein had used Swansea as a *pied à terre* and base for raiding excursions. Moffat's lecture does not appear to have convinced everyone in his audience. An even more enthusiastic proponent of Norse origins for place-names was Dr D.R. Paterson of Cardiff, who proposed Scandinavian origins for places such as Sully (*sulr-ey*, pillar-rock island) and Cardiff (*caer-þýfi*, fort-mound), both of which are now discounted.

9 *The imagined face of Svein Forkbeard, king of Denmark, as depicted at the approach to the Council Chamber, Swansea Guildhall (built 1932-36). Edmund Ernest Morgan, the municipality's architect, advised the Corporation that Moffat's Svein should be officially recognised.*

10 *Illustration by Gertrude Demain Hammond (1862-1952) from Captain Charles Young's* Harald, First of the Vikings *(Harrap, 1930). This was based on the life of Norwegian King Harald Finehair (*Haraldr hárfagri*), from whom Gruffudd ap Cynan claimed descent on his maternal side.*

Charting New Waters

They let out the raines loose to all barbarous cruelty, driving, harrying, spoiling and turning upside down where ever they went (William Camden, 1610).

As if shrouded in a sea mist, only fleeting glimpses of a Scandinavian presence in Wales have been provided as a result of antiquarian study which began in the sixteenth century. Some interpretations they put forward have been discounted on re-examination.

David Powel's *Historie of Cambria* (1584), which was based on the translation of the Welsh Annals by literateur and cartographer Humphrey Llwyd (1527-68), included an account of the Danish raids. The work remained the main authority for the period until J.E. Lloyd's *History of Wales* was published in 1911.

Early studies relied on individuals with a deep regard and opportunity for scholarship. William Camden (1551-1623) viewed the Danes as barbaric sea-warriors, and the first English edition of his *Britannia* (1610) provides lurid descriptions of sacrifices to Thor (*Thur*). Such notions of barbarous swarms of Danish raiders were tempered by more rational scholarship. Later editions of Camden's *Britannia* note of Anglesey, for example, that *Nor was it afterwards harass'd by the English only, but also the Norwegians*. Edward Lhuyd (1660-1709) was Dr Robert Plot's successor as Keeper of the Ashmolean Museum in Oxford. A brilliant scholar, he revised the Welsh entries for Edmund Gibson's new edition of Camden's *Britannia* which appeared in 1695, which included a description of the free-standing tenth-century stone cross known now as '*Maen Achwyfan*' near Whitford, north Wales. His unpublished papers, copied by his assistant William Jones, include an illustration of a similar cross at

Meliden just north of Dyserth, a fragment of which still survives in the Grosvenor Museum, Chester. The topographical writer Richard Fenton (1747-1821) recognised the importance of Scandinavian contact with Wales, and in his *Historical Tour through Pembrokeshire* (1811) he associated many of the earthworks on headlands with 'Danish pirates'.

During the nineteenth century, scholars in Wales focused on the linguistic, literary and historical foundations of national culture. The Danish archaeologist J.J.A. Worsaae (1821-85) visited the

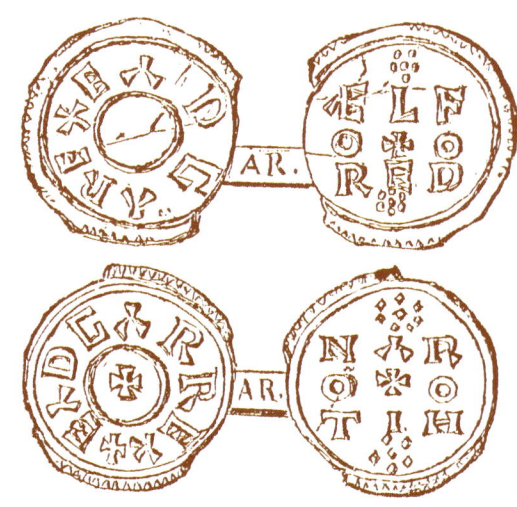

11 *Silver pennies of Edgar (959-75), probably from a small hoard (now lost) found on the site of the old tithe barn near Bangor Cathedral (Vicarage Garden) as published in 1846.*

British Isles in 1846-47 to study its Scandinavian remains. The brevity of his discussion of Wales, which he passed through on his way from Holyhead to Chester, in his book *An Account of the Danes and Norwegians in England, Scotland, and*

12 *The tenth-century cross known as* Maen Achwyfan, *as illustrated in Edmund Gibson's edition of Camden's* Britannia *(1695), which incorporated additions by Lhuyd. In 1695 Edward Lhuyd wrote:* 'When this Monument was erected, or by what Nation, I must leave to farther enquiry.....Dr Plot in his History of Staffordshire [1686] gives us the draughts of a Monument or two, which agree very well with it in the chequer'd carving, and might therefore possibly belong to the same Nation.
Those, he concludes to have been erected by the Danes...' *(p. 830).*

Ireland (1852), reflects perceptions of the time. During this period scholars in Wales worked on the oldest Welsh prose. Dr J. Gwenogvryn Evans (1852-1930) collaborated with Sir John Rhŷs (1840-1915) on the texts of the *Chronicle of the Princes* from the *Red Book of Hergest* (1890), annals which record the first attacks by Vikings on Wales and depict them as 'spoilers of the country'. The tradition concerning the Viking leader Ingimund and his followers in the early tenth century, and their exploits on Anglesey, first became available to students in 1860 with John O'Donovan's publication of the *Annals of Ireland, Three Fragments* by the Irish Archaeological and Celtic Society, Dublin. J. Romilly Allen (1847-1907), member of the Cambrian Archaeological Association from 1875, classified the ornament occurring on pre-Norman sculpture in Wales, including that showing Norse influence. Much of his work continues to influence studies of Viking period decorative stonework.

The nineteenth century has been called an age of rugged individualism, when gifted amateurs and clergymen had the education and means to pursue their personal interests. This included an enthusiasm for the Vikings which spread to Wales. The scholar Connop Thirlwall, Bishop of St David's, subscribed to C.W. Heckethorn's 1856 translation of Bishop Esaias Tegnér's popular Swedish narrative poem *Frithiof's Saga* (1824), which was based on one of the mythical-heroic Icelandic sagas. In 1875 another Bishop of St David's, William Basil Jones, speculated in his inaugural address to the Cambrian Archaeological Association on Scandinavian settlement on the coast and on the shores of Milford Haven: "*Fishgard*" *and* "*Hasgard*", *as well as* "*Skokholm*" *and* "*Skomar*" *have a Danish air about them.* The prolific antiquary Octavius Morgan was aware, from such sources, of the impact of the 'Danes' on the northern shore of the Bristol Channel, which left behind the place-names Steep Holm and Flat Holm. The account he published of

13 *Views like this of St Ann's Head would have been familiar to Viking crews sailing to and from Milford Haven and the south coast of Wales.*

an *Ancient Danish Vessel Discovered at the Mouth of the Usk* (1882) represents one of the first finds in Wales to be attributed to the Vikings. This conclusion was supported by the opinions of the local dock-master, who was familiar with shipbuilding in the Baltic, and may have been influenced by publication in the same year of the spectacular Gokstad Viking ship by the Norwegian State Antiquarian N. Nicolaysen. Morgan read an account of the Gokstad ship in the *Illustrated London News*, and its broad similarities appeared to confirm Morgan's attribution of the Newport find to 'Danish or Northern invaders from the Baltic'. The Newport vessel is now thought to be late eleventh- or twelfth-century in date (p. 60).

Early finds of Viking silver in Wales include a small hoard of coins found in 1845 in the Senior Vicar's garden near the Cathedral at Bangor, the

magnificent armlet hoard from Red Wharf Bay, Anglesey (thought to have been discovered between about 1887 and 1894), and the silver hoard of coins and hack-silver (objects cut up for use as bullion) found in unrecorded circumstances in 1894 on the east of the High Street, Bangor. However, such finds have been few and far between.

Following work in the 1930s by Dr B. G. Charles of the Department of Manuscripts, National Library of Wales, subsequent studies by historians such as Professors Henry Loyn and Wendy Davies have provided a valuable framework for modern research, but until recently archaeologists have had little to show of the Viking period in Wales.

1. Supposed original appearance of the ship, fully equipped.
2. The "King's Hill," where the ship was found.
3. The ship on May 27, after being excavated.
4. Remains of fore-part of sepulchral chamber, seen from the stern.
5. Remains of sepulchral chamber, seen from the stem.
6. Stock of the anchor, 19 ft. or 20 ft. long.
7. The rudder, above 12 ft. long.
8. Oars, 19 ft. or 20 ft. long.
9. Smaller oars, for the small boats found in the ship.
10. Rudder for small boat.
11. Spade, 5 ft. long, somewhat damaged.
12. Remains of a bedstead.

THE NORWEGIAN VIKING SHIP DISCOVERED NEAR SANDEFJORD, NORWAY.

14 *A Norwegian Viking's Ship.*
The discovery of the Gokstad ship in 1880 was reported around the world, and it was to become the archetypal Viking ship of the time. This figure, taken from the Illustrated London News, 24 July 1880, *shows a reconstruction (top left), and the mound in which the ship was found (top right). Scandinavian finds such as this stimulated interest in Viking culture, providing a new view of the legends of the saga writers.*

15 Late eleventh/early twelfth-century cross from St
David's, Pembrokeshire, showing Scandinavian
influence (ECMW 382). The inscription
commemorates the sons of Bishop Abraham, killed in
the Viking raid of 1080.

16 The early tenth-century silver arm-ring hoard from
Red Wharf Bay, Anglesey. External diameters: 65mm,
71mm (3x), 73mm. (NMW 28.215/1-5)

Viking Place-names

Although Viking settlements in Britain have been very difficult to identify, place-names of Scandinavian origin are evidence for the extent of Viking settlement in Britain, Ireland and Normandy. Many such place-names in south Wales, however, probably date from after the Viking period, being introductions by settlers from the Danelaw (the area of northern and eastern England subject to Scandinavian rule) following the Norman Conquest.

The Norse place-names in Wales comprise two main groups. The first are those names which have been preserved for prominent coastal features which were used as navigational points. They are particularly common along the sea route to Bristol, and reflect Norse domination of the seaways and their movements around the coast. For many places, the native inhabitants often retained Welsh names (for example, *Ynys Enlli* for Bardsey Island, *Ynys Môn* for Anglesey). The first group includes the common elements -*holmr* ('islet', 'island') as in Priestholm (*presta* 'priest'-*holmr*, now Puffin Island or *Ynys Seiriol*), Grassholm (*gres* 'grass'-*holmr*), Skokholm (*stokkr* 'pole'-*holmr*), Gateholm (*geit* 'she-goat'-*holmr*), Burry Holms and in the Bristol Channel, Flat Holm and Steep Holm; -*wick* (bay) and -*ford* (fiord) as in Milford Haven (*melr* 'sandbank'-*fjörðr*). Flat Holm, known to the Saxons as *Bradan Relice* ('broad burial-place') became a place of refuge in 1068 for Countess Gytha, mother of Harold (last king of Anglo-Saxon England); in 914 a Viking fleet under earls Hróald and Óttar eventually fled to neighbouring Steep Holm (*Steapan Relice*, 'steep burial-place' to the Saxons), where many perished of hunger. Fishguard has the Scandinavian name *fiskigarðr* ('enclosure for catching or keeping fish'). Other Scandinavian names include the Skerries (*sker*, 'isolated rock'), Emsger, Tusker, the Stacks (*stakkr*, pillar-shaped rock), Stackpole (*stakkr-pollr* 'pool'), Midland (*meðal* 'middle'-*holmr*) and Ormes Head (*örmr* 'snake'). Islands were viewed as targets (if endowed with churches or monasteries) or places of refuge, and the element -*ey* (island) appears a number of times, as in Anglesey (*Önguls-ey*), Bardsey (*Bárð*, personal name,-*ey*), Caldey ('Cold Island'), Skomer (*skálm* 'side of a cleft'-*ey*), Ramsey (either personal name *Hrafns*- or wild garlic *hramsa-ey*), Lundy (*lundi*, 'Puffin' Island) and possibly Swansea (either *Sveinn's-ey* - Svein's island - or -*saer*, 'sea'). In the case of Anglesey, it has been suggested that either the repeated attacks resulted in some limited period of Viking domination, or that the sustained contacts of Gruffudd ap Cynan, prince of Gwynedd (died 1137) and others somehow influenced the description of the island by outsiders. Professor Henry Loyn proposed the temporary establishment of a Scandinavian community on at least part of the island, and that Norse speakers established settlements which were intended to be permanent in Pembrokeshire. Professor Wendy Davies has suggested that Anglesey and Arfon, on either side of the Menai Straits, and Tegeingl (north-east Wales) are possible areas of settlement. Such assessments have relied largely on documentary sources, the annals and Anglo-Norman histories, in which no explicit reference to Viking settlement in Wales can be found, coupled with place-name studies and rare archaeological finds. For example, a Viking burial at Talacre and Viking-inspired ornament on crosses in the same area suggest the existence of an offshoot of settlement in the Wirral and west Cheshire.

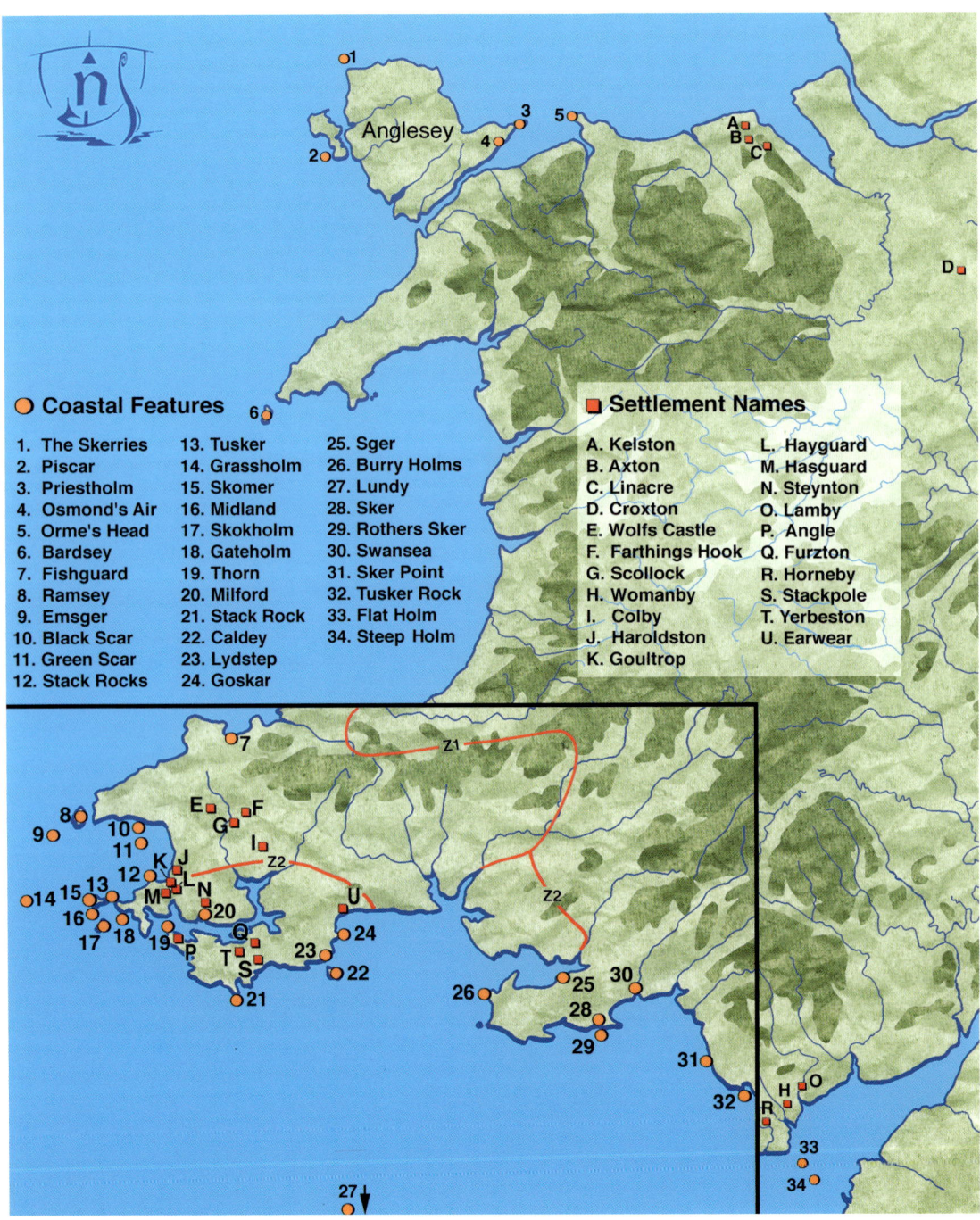

Coastal Features

1. The Skerries
2. Piscar
3. Priestholm
4. Osmond's Air
5. Orme's Head
6. Bardsey
7. Fishguard
8. Ramsey
9. Emsger
10. Black Scar
11. Green Scar
12. Stack Rocks
13. Tusker
14. Grassholm
15. Skomer
16. Midland
17. Skokholm
18. Gateholm
19. Thorn
20. Milford
21. Stack Rock
22. Caldey
23. Lydstep
24. Goskar
25. Sger
26. Burry Holms
27. Lundy
28. Sker
29. Rothers Sker
30. Swansea
31. Sker Point
32. Tusker Rock
33. Flat Holm
34. Steep Holm

Settlement Names

A. Kelston
B. Axton
C. Linacre
D. Croxton
E. Wolfs Castle
F. Farthings Hook
G. Scollock
H. Womanby
I. Colby
J. Haroldston
K. Goultrop
L. Hayguard
M. Hasguard
N. Steynton
O. Lamby
P. Angle
Q. Furzton
R. Horneby
S. Stackpole
T. Yerbeston
U. Earwear

17   Scandinavian place-names in Wales.

18 *Ramsey Island, Pembrokeshire.*

The second group of place-names comprises Scandinavian-style settlement names combined with personal names. Typical examples in England are *-bý* as in Colby in Norfolk ('Col's farmstead'), and Frankby in the Wirral, and *-thorpe* (so-and-so's outlying farm, 'secondary' settlement), both types occurring most frequently in Yorkshire, Nottinghamshire, Lincolnshire and Leicestershire. However, Tenby comes from the Welsh *din-bych*, not the Scandinavian, while Womanby (*hundamannabý*, 'settlement of the dogkeepers') in Cardiff, Momri (*Horn(e)by*, possibly personal name *Horni*) and Lamby (*lang,* 'long') in Monmouthshire are all late in date, and as with such names in the central lowlands of Scotland, may represent settlement from the Danelaw after the Norman Conquest of Wales. In Pembrokeshire, a few names consist of a Scandinavian personal name, followed by the English/Anglo-Saxon element *-tun* such as Furzton (*Thúri*), Haroldston (*Haraldr*), Yerbeston (an anglicised form of *Ásbjorn*), but these are also thought to reflect settlement after the Norman

Conquest by settlers from the areas of England where Danish names were common. Steynton in Pembrokeshire includes the Scandinavian element *steinn* ('stone'). In Flintshire, there is a small cluster of names such as Kelston (*kelda,* 'spring'), Axton (*askr*, 'ash-tree') and possibly Linacre (*lín-akr*) which may represent an infiltration of Scandinavian farmers. Scandinavian elements are also evident in the Pembrokeshire names Goultrop (possibly *göltr,* 'boar' and *hóp*, 'small bay'), Hasguard (*hús-skarth*, 'house in a cleft'), Wolf's Castle (possibly personal name *Ulf*) and Scollock (possibly Scandinavian *skáli* 'hut' and English *hoc*, 'hook').

Interpretation of this evidence depends on when the names were coined. In Wales, native vocabulary was scarcely affected (the few words such as *iarll*, 'earl'; *gardd*, 'garden', could have been introduced through Anglo-Scandinavian or Middle English). Scandinavian place-names only occur in coastal regions. Whilst these place-names entered the English language, some have little linguistic

19 Bardsey Island, off the Lleyn Peninsula. (Crown copyright: Royal Commission on the Ancient and Historical Monuments of Wales)

relationship with the corresponding Welsh names: Bardsey remains Ynys Enlli, Anglesey remains Ynys Môn, Orme's Head remains Penygogarth (suggesting limited contact with the native population).

20 *Midland Isle, with Skomer Island behind and Tusker Rock bottom right.*

21 *Gateholm Island.*

22 *Scandinavians found much metalwork decorated in the indigenous 'Insular' style attractive. This eighth-century pseudo-penannular brooch found at Llys Awel, Pen-y-corddyn-mawr, near Abergele, is similar to brooches found at Eidfjord in Norway and in a Viking grave at Pierowall in Orkney (fitted with a replacement pin in Pictish tradition). Some objects may have travelled north and east through raiding, but trade, ransom and gift-giving are other possibilities. The extent to which native styles were readily adopted by Scandinavians is one area of research today. (NMW 81.35H)*

Viking personal names

Vikings only had one name - a first name such as Svein or Harald which was given by parents. They could be distinguished from each other by the addition of a second name, either that of the father ('patronymic') with the suffix 'son' such as *Eirík Hákonar***son** or 'daughter', such as Thóra Thorsberg**dottir**, or a nickname ('by-name') such as *Haraldr harðráði* - 'Harald Hardruler' - for King Harald Sigurtharson of Norway, killed at the battle of Stamford Bridge in 1066. The Welsh name Rhagnell comes from Norse *Ragnhildr* (as in daughter of Óláf of Dublin and mother of Gruffudd ap Cynan).

For this publication, Old Norse names have been standardised by dropping the nominative endings and simplifying special characters. Some conventional Anglicised forms have been retained.

Viking Blood?

The extent to which Viking people and their culture became integrated into native Welsh society has been a matter of much debate. The term Viking is not a racial label, but a description of what some Scandinavians did. Through archaeology, it is sometimes possible to investigate the degree to which natives and newcomers shared interests, beliefs and tastes. An ethnic group can be defined as a 'people' who set themselves apart on the basis of their own view of their cultural differentiation or common descent. Identifying traces of people with such an awareness of 'Viking' identity in the archaeological record is very difficult, but assessing the relationship between native and mixed Irish/Scandinavian population groups is crucial to our understanding of the period.

Attempts have been made to use the evidence of blood group frequencies of the native population in Wales to identify early immigrant populations, based on data collated by the National Blood Transfusion Service since the 1940s. In general, where history records populations to have a common origin, they have similar blood group frequencies, though the results are averages rather than specific figures. Past studies have shown a high A gene frequency within the indigenous

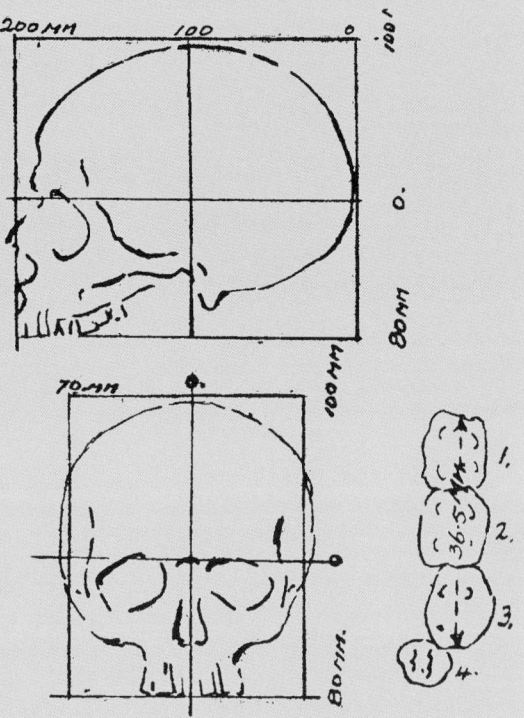

23 *Drawing of the skull of a Viking warrior from a grave at Talacre, Flintshire (reproduced from* Proceedings of the Llandudno, Colwyn Bay and District Field Club *17, 1931-32).*

population of Pembrokeshire, and interesting levels in the north-west. Analysis showed a large difference between Pembrokeshire and the rest of Wales only matched by some parts of Scandinavia, the atypical area being north Pembrokeshire (see figure 17, Z1) and not south (Z2). Some have viewed this as a reflection of settlement of Norse origin and intermarriage, leaving slight traces over thirty or more generations. However, in strict archaeological terms it is not yet possible to demonstrate that Scandinavians formed a significant element of the permanent population. The Pembrokeshire statistics contrast with that of Anglesey, the other likely area for limited settlement. In Normandy no corresponding high frequency of A genes has been recorded, although some of the ruling elite was Norse in origin. Caution is required in interpreting the data, and the effects of natural selection, chance effects such as genetic drift and other influences need to be considered. More sophisticated methods of analysis have now been developed but have limitations (mitochondrial DNA being only transmitted in the female line). Any attempts to identify a Viking or Scandinavian component within the population's blood must await the completion of detailed programmes of genetic mapping of males and females in Britain.

The Native Kingdoms

In the ninth century, Wales consisted of a number of independent kingdoms, ruled by kings such as Cyngen, last king of Powys. When he died in 856, his kingdom was absorbed into Gwynedd. The expansion of Gwynedd under Rhodri ap Merfyn – better known as Rhodri Mawr (844-78) – and his princely sons, was soon undermined by Viking raids and internal divisions. In the tenth century Rhodri's grandson, Hywel ap Cadell, united Seisyllwg in Deheubarth with Gwynedd. Known as Hywel Dda ('the Good'; c. 920-50), he was a key figure in the political development of Wales.

While the courts (*llysoedd*) and monastic centres of eighth- to tenth-century Wales were prominent and are sometimes recorded in the historical record, archaeological evidence for them is difficult to find. In the kingdom of Gwynedd, Aberffraw on Anglesey was the chief seat or *llys* of the kingdom. Other 'high status' sites have been identified at Degannwy and Dinas Emrys, but undefended farmsteads and peasant homes are only found by chance.

The independent kingdoms were united in part by the Christian religion. The church was supported

24   *The cross probably set up by Hywel ap Rhys, ruler of Glywysing, 'for the soul of his father',* from Llantwit Major, Vale of Glamorgan (ECMW 220). Hywel, subject of Alfred the Great in the 870s, died in 886. (Cast; NMW 99.64)

25   *The fortified western hillock at Degannwy is thought to be the site of arx Decantorum (the citadel of the Decanti) which, according to the Welsh annals, was struck by lightning and burnt down in 812. In 823 it was destroyed by Saxons who took over the kingdom of Powys. Later in the late eleventh century, the Norman Robert of Rhuddlan erected a castle on the site, which was later rebuilt in stone (now represented only by fragments of masonry straddling the two hillocks). The wooded hill (top left) is Bryn Maelgwyn, on whose slopes a coin hoard was deposited c. 1024.*

The original
territories of
the ruler

The additional
territories brought
under his rule

Llanbedrgoch

Aberffraw

Degannwy

Rhuddlan

GWYNEDD
844

Offa's Dyke

Mathrafal

× Buttington

POWYS
855

Ceredigion

Maelienydd

Buellt

Elfael

SEISYLLWG
871/2

DYFED

Brycheiniog

GWENT

Dinefwr

Llan-gors

Glywysing

MORGANNWG

Rhodri Mawr
844 - 878

26   *The changing political structure of Wales under Rhodri Mawr. Few kingdoms were
continuously dominant (based on William Rees 1951).*

by the ruling elite, and some monasteries became
burial grounds for the royal houses. The larger
monasteries were centres of learning and
craftsmanship, and from the ninth century this was
reflected in the tradition of erecting elaborate high
crosses, taking the form of a tall slab or cross
sculptured in the round. The localised distribution
of these cross types, often centred on early

Llanbedrgoch

Aberffraw

Degannwy   Rhuddlan

GWYNEDD
942

Offa's Dyke

The original
territories of
the ruler

The additional
territories brought
under his rule

POWYS
942

Maelienydd

SEISYLLWG
c. 900

Buellt

Elfael

DYFED
c. 904

c.930
Brycheiniog

GWENT

Llan-gors

Glywysing

MORGANNWG

Hywel Dda

c.900 - 950

27   *Wales under Hywel Dda (based on William Rees 1951).*

ecclesiastical sites such as St David's, Pembrokeshire, and Llantwit Major, Vale of Glamorgan, suggests the existence of workshops or groups of craftsmen under the patronage of wealthy monasteries or royal rulers. By the ninth century, many monasteries had become wealthy, and were clear targets for Viking attacks.

The First Coming

'... Never before has such a terror appeared in Britain as we have now suffered from a pagan race, nor was it thought possible that such an inroad from the sea could be made.'

(letter from the scholar Alcuin to the king of Northumbria on the raid on Lindisfarne, AD 793; translation by D. Whitelock).

The impact of the first Viking raids in the late eighth and ninth centuries by highly mobile war bands – led by middle ranking warriors (often landowners or local chieftains), rather than kings, princes or *iarls* – was profound.

The first recorded raids on Britain and Ireland appear to have taken place at the end of the eighth century. Three ships from *Hörthaland* (Hordaland, Norway) landed at Portland, Dorset, during the reign of king Beorhtric *c.* 789 and killed the king's reeve (possibly a trading venture which came to grief). Monasteries were attacked at Lindisfarne in 793; *Rechru*, probably Rathlin Island, Co. Antrim in 795 and Iona in the same year. The contemporary records are imperfect because they are primarily ecclesiastical and the concise annals distort the past by omission. Consequently there were probably more raids that went unrecorded. Nevertheless, following the late eighth-century shift from Scandinavian trade to attack, a general pattern of increasing raids followed by periods of relative security is evident. The mid-ninth century saw overwintering of Viking raiders in Ireland, the establishment of a naval encampment or *longphor*t at Dublin in 841, the development of a Viking presence on both sides of the Irish Sea, and intermarriage and alliances between Irish and Norse. The Scandinavian

28 *Early Viking raids on Wales.*

kingdom based on York (which they seized in 867) was established by 876.

The first definite recorded raid on Wales was in 852, when Cyngen of Powys was slain by Vikings (*Gentiles*), and Anglesey (then Môn) was a particular target from 855. Sporadic probing raids in the north and south, which occurred until about 919, have been described as a 'backwash' of Viking activity, for their efforts were actually focused elsewhere. Their effective repulsion was no doubt aided by geography, a hazardous coastline and political circumstances. Rhodri Mawr (Rhodri the Great), ruler of Gwynedd from 844-78, led the

initial resistance, his successes being noted in Ireland (in the *Annals of Ulster*) and at the court of Charles the Bald at Liège. His successors were also effective in resisting Viking raids. In 903 Vikings led by Ingimund came to Anglesey after their expulsion from Dublin. Expelled again by the Welsh king Clydog son of Cadell, they sailed east and were allowed to land near Chester, which marked an important stage in the settlement of north-west England.

The initial raids took place in the summer only, but by the mid-ninth century Vikings were settling in northern Scotland and were regularly encamped during the winter in both Ireland and England. According to the Welsh scholar Asser, writing his *Life of Alfred the Great* in 893 shortly after these events, a Viking force (led, according to later tradition, by Hubba, brother of Ívar the Boneless (*Hinn Beinlausi*) and Hálfdan of the Wide Embrace)

29 *This eighth-century gilt bronze cruciform mount from the Wye Valley, Monmouthshire, has Anglo-Saxon chip-carved decoration in the form of vine tendril interlace. Two rivets once fastened it to a book cover. A similar mount, converted to a pendant, was found in a woman's grave at Björke, Norway. Some of the 'Insular' (British) metalwork found in Norway may have been plundered through raiding (particularly those items deposited in graves dated to the eighth century), while other items may have been traded. Maximum arm width 65.6mm.*

30 *The first phase of Viking presence around Wales is marked by the burial of hoards. These coins, shown here in an uncleaned state, are from a small hoard deposited about 850 at Llanbedrgoch, Anglesey. They include mostly Carolingian coins - deniers of Charles the Bald (struck c. 848-77), Pepin II of Aquitaine (839-52) and Louis the Pious (struck c. 822-40) - and the hoard is of a similar composition to another small hoard from Minchin Hole on the Gower Peninsula.*

overwintered in 878 in Dyfed (probably for the first time) where they slaughtered a large number of Christians. Asser and Æthelweard record that the Viking fleet of twenty-three ships then sailed to Devon, possibly as part of a pincer movement to trap Alfred who was hiding with his supporters in the Somerset fenlands. The Vikings were eventually defeated by local militia under Ealdorman Odda before the hillfort at Countisbury Hill near Minehead. According to Asser, apart from its ramparts 'built in Welsh manner', the site was unfortified.

Following the death of the charismatic Alfred in 899, his son Edward the Elder (899-924), his son-in-law Æthelræd of Mercia and his daughter Æthelflæd (married to Æthelræd) continued the campaign to conquer the Danelaw territories until 918, by which time a generation of Danish farmers and families had grown up and worked the land in the north and east of England. There were instances of military co-operation between the Welsh and West Saxons against the Vikings, as illustrated by the events of 914. A Viking fleet from Brittany, led by Earls Hróald (Harold) and Óttar, ravaged the coast of south Wales and penetrated the Wye Valley. They even captured Cyfeiliog,

Bishop of Ergyng (Archenfield), and took him to their ships. According to the *Anglo-Saxon Chronicle*, it was Edward the Elder who paid *xl. pundum*, 'forty pounds' (of silver) in ransom for him. Repulsed by the combined garrison forces of Hereford and Gloucester, the Vikings eventually fled to Steep Holm in the Bristol Channel, where many died of hunger: *hie wurdon swiþe metelease* ('until they were meatless'; *Anglo-Saxon Chronicle*). The Viking practice of carrying only limited provisions and living off the land could be disastrous. From Steep Holm they eventually sailed to Dyfed (probably the Milford Haven area) and Ireland.

31 *Raiding in Wales was by no means restricted to Vikings. This graph shows the frequency of hostilities recorded in the annals. While the annals provide only a partial record of what actually happened, it is clear that the raids by Viking marauders represent but one element of a complex pattern of military expeditions and warring bands. Internal and intra-national violence may have contributed to Viking interest in Wales. The initial phase of their raiding corresponds with the first 'Viking Age' in North Britain c. 795-920.*

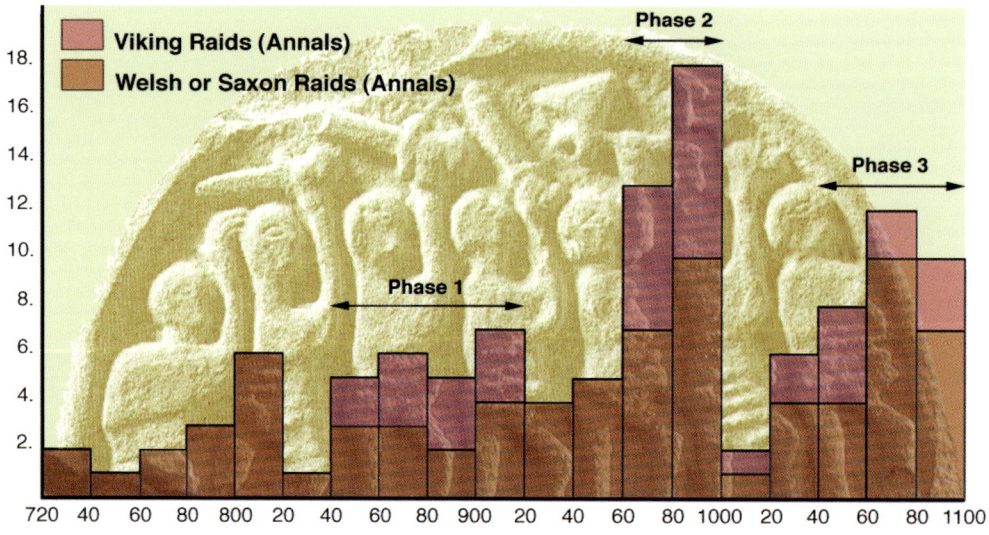

32 *Copper alloy knobbed ringed pin from Caerwent, Monmouthshire. This is the only example known from Wales, and probably of ninth-century date. The pin shaft, which is of rectangular cross-section, is decorated with three incised saltires. Surviving length 126mm. (Newport Museum & Art Gallery; NPTMG: D2.250)*

33 *Rhodri Mawr shown in classical Renaissance style, in David Powel's* The Historie of Cambria *(1584). The image was borrowed from Holinshed's* Chronicles of England *(1577).*

The Battle of Buttington

'These things done at Buttington are still proclaimed by old men.'

(from the Chronicle of Æthelweard, written in 980s)

The Viking campaigns of the 890s were a consequence of a large Viking army landing in England (after encountering growing resistance on the Continent) and were associated with attempts to overthrow Alfred's kingdom. In 893, the Viking leader Hástein broke treaty. His large force, reinforced by Danish armies from East Anglia and Northumbria, ravaged the midland kingdom of Mercia along the Thames valley, until it came to the borders of the Welsh (*Britannorum*). They then marched up the Severn valley, but that summer an English force assembled from *burhs* (fortifications, many 'townships') in the west of England combined with the Welsh and overtook them from the rear at Buttington. This is generally thought, since at least 1833, to have been the village on the banks of the

Severn near Welshpool (Montgomery). Alternative sites at Boddington, near Cheltenham, and Buttington-hill, opposite Chepstow, in Gloucestershire have also been suggested for the encounter, but the *Chronicle's* statement that the Danes reached Buttington after moving *up be Sæferne*, 'up the Severn', pursued by mounted infantry favours the Montgomeryshire site. Manuscript A of the *Anglo-Saxon Chronicle* states *þā offōron hīe þone here hindan æt Buttingtūne on Sæferne staþe*, 'then they overtook the Danish army at Buttington, on the bank of the Severn'.

The encounter is notable for the co-operation between Saxons and Welsh. For many weeks, this large combined English and Welsh force, led by three of Alfred's provincial governors, besieged

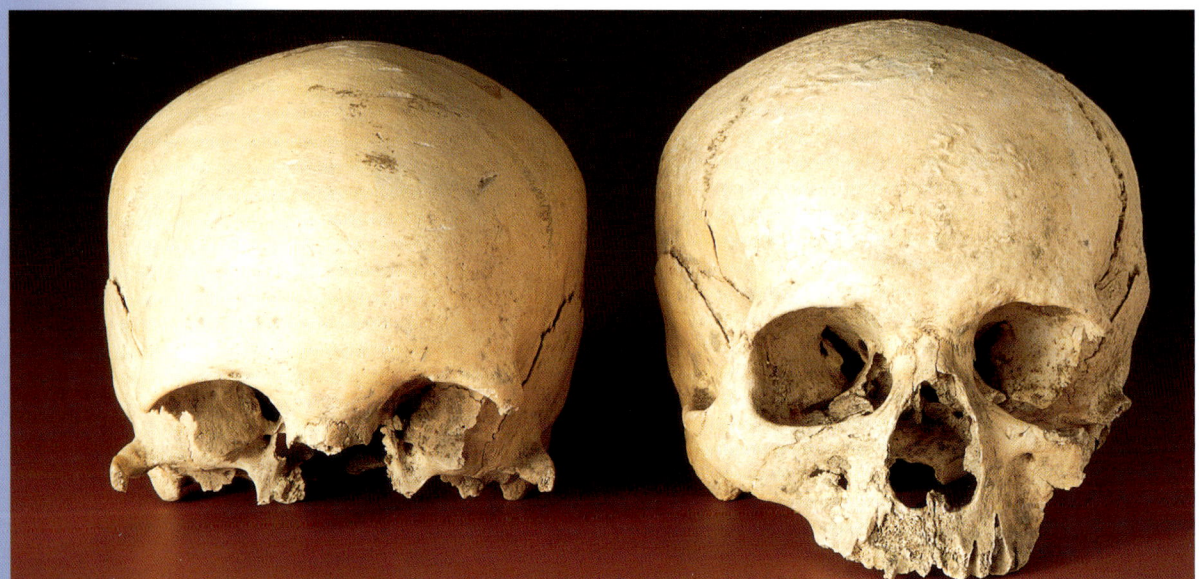

34 *Are these the skulls of Danes? They are reputed to have come from the charnel pits at Buttington churchyard. The skulls are now at Powysland Museum & Montgomeryshire Canal Centre.*

35 *Buttington churchyard, showing the slight elevation above the flood-plain and the Long Mountain rising in the background*

36 *Buttington churchyard. The charnel pits were discovered during the excavation of foundations for the school house in 1838 (beneath the left-hand corner of the brick building in the photograph).*

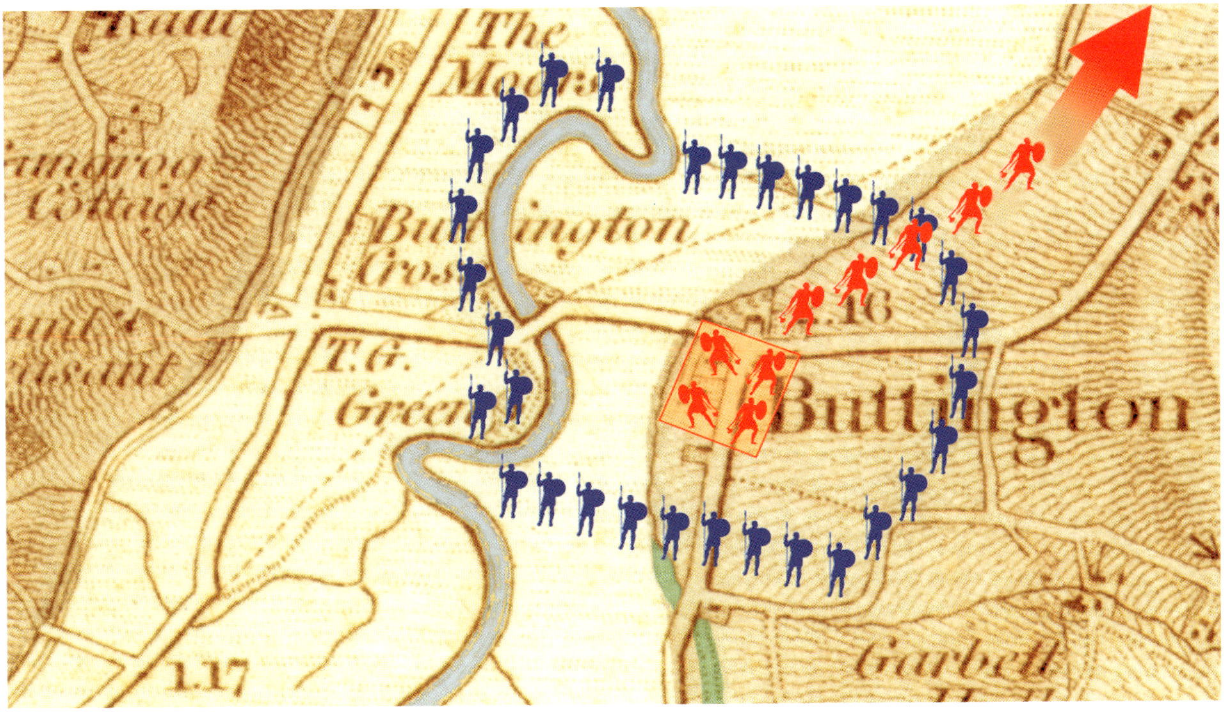

37 *A possible interpretation of the battle of Buttington. The ford gave access through Offa's Dyke from Mercian territory across the River Severn, and ancient roads and tracks lead to it from both sides of the river. The construction of the railway in the nineteenth century changed the character of the site, and there are now no signs of defences or 'strong works' around the raised area of the church, such as the 'rampart' noted in the 1870s on the east side of the church, running almost parallel with the road to Forden. Although the site of a rectangular fortification about 120m x 170m in size has been proposed, it remains unproven.*

Hástein's Danish camp set up at Buttington, *[ond] þǣr ūtan besǣton on ǣlce healfe on ānum fæstenne,* 'and besieged them on both sides of the river in a fortress' (from Manuscript A of the *Anglo-Saxon Chronicle*). This description does not conflict with the topography of the proposed site at Buttington churchyard, though clear archaeological evidence for any defensive system remains to be found. A rapidly erected fortification of earth and timber may well have made use of pre-existing features. The besieging force completely surrounded the Danes occupying both banks, the west bank probably being covered by a Welsh force under Merfyn of Powys, which thereby avoided any risk of being trapped in a counter-attack against the Severn on the east flood-plain. The Danes were prevented from their customary habit of living off the land, and as supplies dwindled, they were reduced to eating their horses, some men dying of starvation. In desperation some broke out against the force on the east side of the river, presumably a shield-wall of Saxons. According to Æthelweard, 'The youth of the English afterwards gained the field of victory', and the Danes were defeated with heavy losses on both sides, the surviving Danes fleeing to East Anglia. Though a notable allied success, the invaders were not decisively defeated, for the Great Army then made secure its property in East Anglia, reassembled, and made a rapid march to Chester. The English forces destroyed their food sources, forcing them to move into Wales for supplies in 894, perhaps devastating

38 *A reaction to turbulent times? Llan-gors crannog was an artificial island built in a lake as a royal* llys *for the king of Brycheiniog, Elisedd ap Tewdwr. The blackened oak planks seen here under excavation in 1990 (in the foreground) once formed a high palisade around the crannog. Some were fashioned from oaks felled in the summer of 893, the same year as the battle of Buttington.*

the kingdoms of Brycheiniog, Gwent and Gwynllwg during this expedition. They then turned back from Wales 'with the booty they had seized there' (*Anglo-Saxon Chronicle*) and returned to East Anglia by way of Northumbria.

In 1838, about 400 skulls and other assorted bones were found in three pits buried in the churchyard at Buttington. The bones were interpreted at the time as the remains of Danes which had later been reburied in charnel pits by the monks of Strata Marcella Abbey. This recalls the similar quantity of human bone stacked charnel-wise in a mass burial excavated below a mound at Repton, Derbyshire, site of the winter camp of the Great Army in 873-74. Some of the Buttington teeth were sold at sixpence and a shilling apiece by the workmen – a local remedy against toothache - but most of the bones were reinterred on the north side of the churchyard. According to the antiquary W. Boyd Dawkins (1873), some skulls had been fractured, but there is no mention in his description of blade cuts, and post-mortem damage is a possible cause. Whether they actually are the remains of Hastein's Danes (or others) is not known. The ford over the Severn known as *Rhyd-y-groes* ('Ford of the Cross'), site of Gruffudd ap Llywelyn's victory over the 'Saxons and other Gentiles' in 1039, is also thought to lie near Buttington.

39 *A semi-submerged section of palisade planking on the south side of Llan-gors crannog.*

A Siege at Chester

After his expulsion from Dublin and then Anglesey (902-3), Ingimund travelled eastwards, and was eventually granted some land near Chester by Æthelflæd, 'Lady of the Mercians' and King Alfred's daughter, who was married to Ealdorman Æthelræd of Mercia. A story recorded in the Irish annals conjures up a vivid image of this heathen Viking. Seeing the wealth of the city, Ingimund conspired with the chiefs of the Norse and Danes to seize Chester if not granted more land and wealth. When they attacked the town some time between 903 and 911, the inhabitants were prepared. Those outside the walls feigned a retreat into the town, and the gates were only closed after a large force of pursuing Norsemen had entered. Trapped, these Norsemen were slaughtered. The Irish among the 'pagans' were urged to change sides and betray the Danes. A manuscript source, known as *The Three Fragments*, provides a detailed account of what happened:

'But the other forces, the Norsemen, were under the hurdles piercing the walls. What the Saxons and the Irishmen who were among them did was to throw large rocks so that they destroyed the hurdles over them. What they did in the face of this was to place large posts under the hurdles. What the Saxons did was to put all the ale and water of the town in the cauldrons of the town, to boil them and pour them over those who were under the hurdles so that their skins were stripped from them. The answer which the Norsemen gave to this was to spread hides on the hurdles. What the Saxons did was to let loose on the attacking force all the beehives in the town, so that they could not move their legs or hands from the great number of bees stinging them.

Afterwards they left the city and abandoned it. It was not long after that [before they came] to wage battle again'.
(*Annals of Ireland*; translation by I.Ll. Foster)

This lively account has a legendary flavour, and one cannot have much confidence in the detail: the source has been described as a 'modernised collection of largely legendary material based on John O'Donovan's nineteenth-century copy of a transcript made in 1643 ... from a now lost

40 *Reconstruction of Chester in the tenth century, viewed from the south-west. The Roman defences, which remained largely intact, may have been extended to the river, and settlement is shown in the Lower Bridge Street area. (Drawing by D.P. Astley and A.M. Beckett; copyright Chester City Council. Reproduced with permission)*

fragmentary manuscript, the date and provenance of which are unknown'. Nonetheless, some of the story may have a basis in historical fact. The Mercian defenders had successfully repulsed the attack. As a peace gesture, Æthelflæd granted Ingimund some land, thought to have been in the northern half of the Wirral Peninsula, an area which has a dense concentration of Norse place-names. Other Norse settlement appears to have occurred along the north side of the Mersey, and there are a few place-names around Chester and along the coast of Flintshire.

Chester Rediscovered

Alfred the Great and his successors established a network of fortifications called *burhs*, which were central to the defence against the Danes. These ranged from hillforts to walled towns. Chester had been seized and used by Danish raiders from East Anglia in 893 after the battle of Buttington, but they were soon expelled. A *burh* or defended enclave was established by Æthelflæd at this strategically situated town in 907, possibly in response to the Viking siege of Chester. A number of *burhs* were created near the border with Wales at Tamworth (913), Stafford (913), Chirbury near Buttington (915), Hereford and Gloucester at about the same time, and in 921 *Cledemutha*, usually identified as Rhuddlan near Rhyl. Chester defended north-west Mercia.

The *burh* defences certainly re-used the northern and eastern sides of the Roman fortress and may have extended them to the river. Several late Saxon domestic structures have been excavated, which include sunken-floored buildings and rectangular structures of several kinds: hall-type buildings, open-sided timber framed buildings and those of basement design. The remains of rectangular buildings with basements or semi-basements just outside the old fortress walls in what is now Lower Bridge Street have been interpreted by the excavators as evidence for a Viking community. If true,

41 Nine coins from the Chester hoard, found at St John's Church in 1862, and buried c. 917. One Norse moneyer operating under Edward the Elder was called Irfara *or 'Ireland journeyer'. (NMW 85.72H)*

Legend

- — · — · **Reuse of Roman wall?**
- — ● — ● **Extension to Saxon burh?**
- — — — **Roman fortress wall**
- ——— **Roman fortress wall (reused)**
- □ □ □ **10th century buildings**
- ● **Hoards**

St Werburgh's †

St Peter's †

Wolfeld Gate

St John's †

St Bridget's †

St Olave's †

Norman castle

River Dee

n̂

0 ———— 300m

42 Chester during the tenth century. The town was occupied by Danish Scandinavians from England in 893, but they were soon expelled. It was not until the tenth century that any form of permanent settlement was established, and Chester became an economic partner with Dublin.

there is little evidence for the segregation of Scandinavian and Saxon communities, for Viking artefacts have been found in the supposed Saxon part of the settlement. A large hoard of Viking silver, buried about 965, has been found in the city (Castle Esplanade), and a church dedicated to St Olave (the Norwegian King Olaf martyred in 1030) still stands in Lower Bridge Street. Close by also stood the 'Wolfeld Gate', an Anglicisation of the Old Norse name *Ulfaldi's* gate, probably named after a man with such a nickname who was prominent in Chester's affairs, perhaps in the tenth or eleventh century. St John's church, just to the east of the city walls outside the Wolfeld Gate near Lower Bridge Street, has an important collection of stone sculpture (grave-markers) in Anglo-Scandinavian style.

The Second Phase

'With their hammered blades, the sons of Edward
Clove the shield-wall and hacked the linden bucklers,
As was instinctive in them, from their ancestry,
To defend their land, their treasures and their homes...'
(Anglo-Saxon Chronicle *on the battle of Brunanburh, 937*)

Viking raiding declined during the first half of the tenth century, as groups began to settle in north and east England. Warriors were now organised into armies of seasoned campaigners and paid mercenaries.

Between 919 and 950, while the Vikings were engaged in Normandy and the Danelaw, good relations and co-operation between Hywel Dda of Deheubarth and the House of Wessex contributed to a period of security and unity against a common Viking threat. It was also during this period that Viking links between Dublin, York and the Isle of Man were consolidated.

Hywel Dda frequented the court of Alfred's grandson Æthelstan (924-39) 'Basileus of the English', who imposed a heavy annual demand for tribute on north Wales which according to William of Malmesbury's late account comprised 20 pounds of gold, 300 pounds of silver, 25,000 oxen, hounds and hawks. Much to the delight of the Irish and

Franks, Æthelstan defeated the alliance of Scots and Dublin Norse under Óláf Guthfrithsson (Anlaf) in 937 at the battle of *Brunanburh*, an unidentified site thought by some to lie in Cheshire on the Wirral at

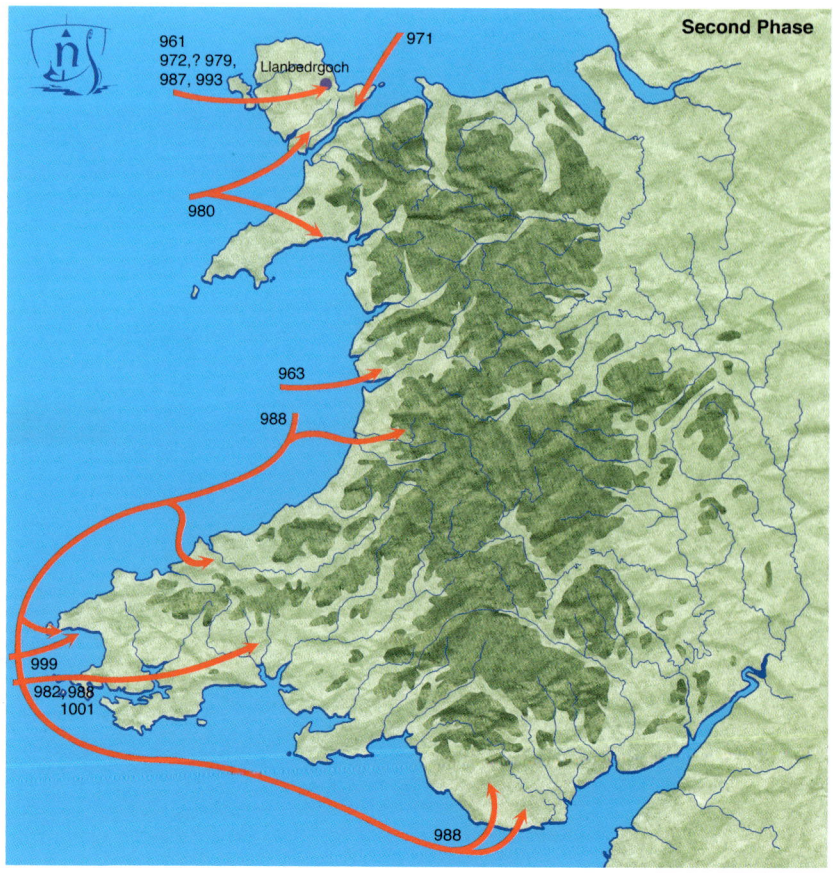

43   *The second phase of Viking raids on Wales.*

44 *King Edgar depicted offering the Charter of the New Minster, Winchester, to Christ. (London, British Library, Cotton. Ms Vespasian A. viii, fol. 2v. By permission of The British Library)*

45 *Obverse and reverse of a coin of Edgar, who was responsible for reforming and unifying Anglo-Saxon coinage. (NMW 55.553/3)*

46 *Hywel Dda, as portrayed in David Powel's* Historie of Cambria *(1584). It is in fact the portrait of Henry II used in Holinshed's* Chronicles of England *(1577).*

47 *The so-called Hywel Dda penny, produced by the moneyer* Gillys *in Chester (replica from original in the British Museum). Wales had no coinage of its own, and Welsh hoards contain coins minted in England, the Middle East and on the Continent. (NMW 60.375)*

Bromborough (the vanquished escaped to Dublin). Other sites for the battle have been proposed, including Burnswark in Annandale (near the Solway Firth), Brinksworth in Yorkshire and the Forest of Bromswald on the borders of Northamptonshire and Huntingdonshire. This important battle, recorded by the English, Irish and Welsh annals, is also described in the later saga of Egil Skallagrímsson, who, together with his brother Thorolf, was in charge of the Viking troops in the service of the English king.

48 *St David's (Menevia), site of a monastery which became the main cult centre of Dewi. It was subjected to frequent Viking attacks. In 999, the Norse slew Bishop Morgeneu, and in 1080 Bishop Abraham was slain by Gentiles.*

49 Iron prick spur from Rhuddlan, Denbighshire. The straight tapering neck ends in a moulding and a small pointed goad; there are two ring terminals for attachment to leather. Similar spurs from Viking Dublin have been found in deposits dated to c. 1025-50. Overall length 107mm. Probably early eleventh century. (NMW 96.9H)

The mention of 'Welsh' leaders (Adils and Hingr) on the side of the Viking/Scottish coalition may derive from a tradition of support by the kingdom of Strathclyde (in south-west Scotland), or a confusion with later events: Idwal of Gwynedd, who had paid tribute to king Æthelstan, rebelled in 942 against Edmund.

Hywel Dda's pragmatic policy of co-operation contrasts with the passionate sentiments expressed in a famous dissident poem in Welsh composed possibly by a monk from south Wales about 930, known as *Armes Prydein* ('The Prophecy of Britain'), which called upon the Scandinavians to help the Welsh and other Britons in a coalition to expel the English from the Island of Britain. This may have been a reaction to the size of Welsh tribute exacted by Æthelstan at Hereford.

A gynhon Dulyn genhyn y safant.
pan dyffont yr gat nyt ymwadant.
'And Dublin's clansmen will stand beside us;
When they come to the field they will not play false'.
(translation by J.P. Clancy, 1970)

King Edgar (959-75) succeeded in keeping England united and secure from invaders for sixteen years. Shortly after his late coronation in Bath in 973 he sailed around Wales to Chester, where eight kings (including Hywel ap Idwal and the king of Man, Maccus (Magnús)) are said to have acknowledged his supremacy by symbolically rowing him on the River Dee while he held the rudder.

The so-called 'Second Viking Age' in Wales started about 950, following the death of Hywel Dda. The peace fostered by king Edgar did not extend consistently to Wales. The renewal of attacks coincided with an increase in civil strife, and the expulsion of Eirík Bloodaxe from York in 954. There were numerous raids on the coastal lowlands, and in particular monasteries, such as those at Penmon and Caer Gybi near Holyhead (Anglesey), Tywyn (Gwynedd), St David's (eleven times between 967 and 1091), Clynnog Fawr (978) and St Dogmaels (Pembrokeshire), Llanbadarn Fawr (Ceredigion), Llantwit Major and Llancarfan (Vale of Glamorgan). However, to judge from the documentary records, which may be incomplete, Welsh churches appear to have suffered lightly in comparison with the fate of those in Ireland. Many of the raiders were based in Ireland, Man (such as Guthröth) or the Hebrides. In 987 south Wales suffered attacks from an army which operated until 1002, when it was paid off with tribute in silver (known in Old English as *gafol*).

According to the history of Gruffudd ap Cynan, his grandfather Óláf Sihtricsson, king of Dublin, built a fortification known as 'Olaf's Castle' or 'Bon y Dom' in Gwynedd. This site is, as yet, unidentified.

Rhuddlan

Rhuddlan is generally thought to be the location of the *burh* known as *Cledemutha* established in 921 by Edward the Elder, bringing north-east Wales under direct English political control. Excavations here have uncovered sunken-floored buildings and tenth-century hearths. Whether the earthworks to the south of the motte are those of the Anglo-Saxon *burh* remain the subject of debate. It is unclear whether Rhuddlan at this period was a large regional centre, or a small enclave dependant on its port, border traffic and nearby estates. While Rhuddlan and the other *burhs* are traditionally viewed as a response to Viking incursions in the early tenth century, they may also have been concerned with problems associated with the Welsh border (in the case of Rhuddlan as a frontier port) and the disloyalty of the local population, as well as playing a part in a Mercian policy of territorial expansion. Rhuddlan became the seat and *llys* of Gruffudd ap Llywelyn in the eleventh century, but was destroyed by Harold Godwinesson in the winter campaign of 1062.

50 *Plan of Rhuddlan* (Cledemutha?), *which was probably founded in 921 to ensure local control and curb Viking infiltration.*

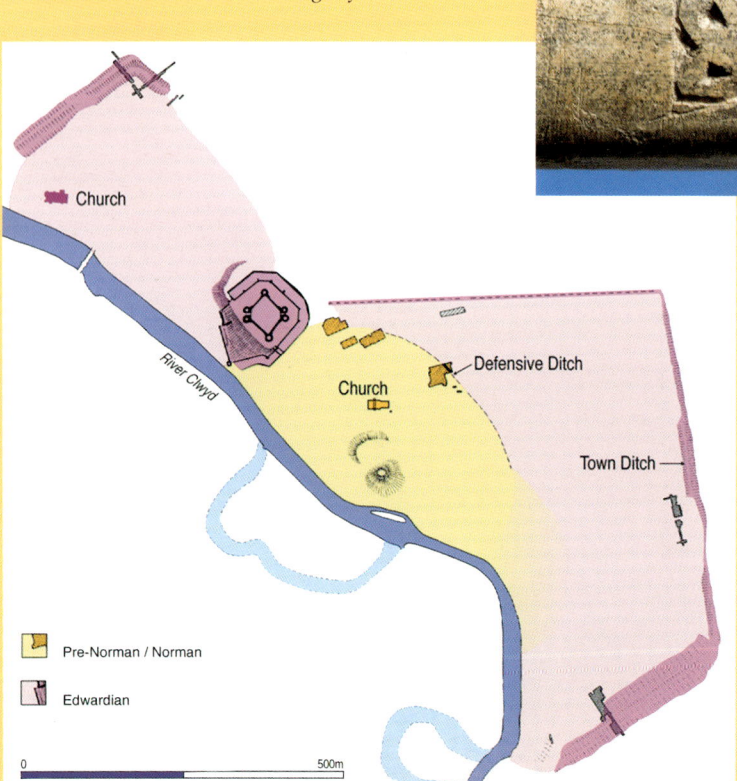

51 *Unfinished design, known as a 'motif piece', from Rhuddlan, Denbighshire. It is roughly incised on a radial bone of a calf and depicts a beast in Anglo-Scandinavian style and interlace. Bones were often used by craftsmen to practise intricate designs. Design length 43.2mm. (NMW 96.9H)*

Church

River Clwyd

Defensive Ditch

Church

Town Ditch

Pre-Norman / Norman

Edwardian

0   500m

Öngul's Isle

It is on Anglesey that the evidence for Vikings is, perhaps, strongest. The fertile, undulating, arable and pasture fields which form most of the island's landscape provide a dramatic contrast to the rugged high-peaked massif of Snowdonia on the mainland. It has a rocky coastline, indented with numerous small headlands and coves, and some larger bays. On its west side rises Holyhead Mountain (height 220m), from which the Isle of Man and the Wicklow mountains can be seen on clear days. Unlike much of north Wales, the island's topography and location (situated a comfortable sailing distance from Scandinavian settlements to west, north and east) combined with political factors to bring it into the Hiberno-Norse world. Lying about 65 miles (105 km) from Dublin,

Afrike, Italie, **and other hot regions.**

9 0 0   **About the yeare** 9 0 0. Igmond **with a great number of souldiours came to** Anglesey, **and the** Welshmen **gaue him battell at** Molerain.

✻ There be some Brytish copies of this historie, which affirme, that this battell betweene Igmond captaine of the blacke nations and the Brytaines, wherein Mervyn was slaine, was fought at a place called Meilon, of the which it was called Maes Rhos Meilon.

52 From page 42 of David Powel's The Historie of Cambria, *1584.*

Anglesey was a target for numerous raids, as well as trade. Red Wharf Bay on the north-eastern coastline provided an obvious landfall and sheltered haven for those sailing between Dublin and Chester, and a likely landing place for Viking leader Ingimund. When he landed in 903, he and his followers held *Maes Ros Meilon*, thought to be Osfeilion (arguably on the Penmon peninsula). According to the Irish and Welsh annals they were forcibly expelled by the Welsh leader Clydog.

Scandinavian familiarity with the island is demonstrated by the place-names of Scandinavian origin which have been given to prominent features: *Önguls-ey* is traditionally thought to incorporate a personal name – presumably a Viking

53   *In the sagas and other sources, distances between points were often reckoned by the Norse in terms of a 'day's sailing'* (doegr-sigling). *The precise meaning of this term is controversial: while it refers to a period of time, it may signify a unit of distance. The* **half-doegr**, *possibly a period of 12 hours, has been equated with a distance of 72 nautical miles (shown here centred on Red Wharf Bay). The strategic importance of Anglesey, at the hub of the southern Irish Sea, is clear when radii for a* **half-doegr** *are plotted from the Isle of Man, Dublin, Chester and the Wirral; all arcs intersect in Anglesey waters. This does not indicate the speed of a vessel or the actual time of a voyage. The average speed for a Norse ship might vary from 3.5 - 8 knots, which would make a passage from Anglesey to Dublin between 12 and 25 hours sailing time.*

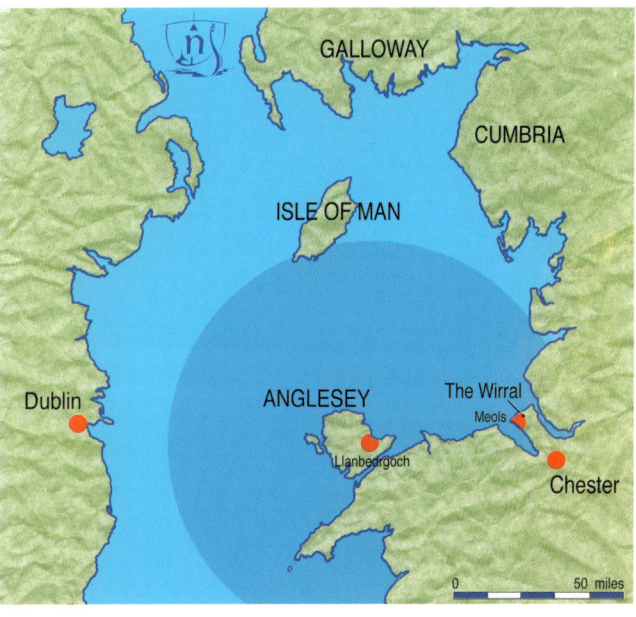

leader – and a settlement of some sort has been assumed on part of the island. *The Skerries, Piscar, Priestholm* and *Osmond's Air* near Beaumaris (from *Asmundr* and *eyrr* 'a gravel bank near the sea') are all coastal features.

Anglesey in the ninth and tenth centuries was the favoured economic and political homeland of the kingdom of Gwynedd, with a royal *llys* at Aberffraw, monasteries at Penmon and Caer Gybi and a host of churches administering to its Christian population.

54 *'Viking Age' Anglesey. In 968 even Aberffraw, traditionally one of the three 'tribal thrones of the Island of Britain' and probably principal royal court* (llys) *of Gwynedd, was attacked by Vikings.*

55 *Isolated finds include this Anglo-Saxon silver penny of Edward the Martyr (975-78) found close to the inside face of the Roman fort wall at Caer Gybi, Holyhead, Anglesey. This is the site of St Cybi's church, which was raided by Vikings in 961. The coin could have been an offering to the early church or accidental loss, perhaps reflecting commercial activity in the vicinity of the monastery. (NMW 70.42H/1)*

Viking and Native Politics

The displacement of Viking leaders from Dublin in the early tenth century had repercussions around the Irish Sea, so that by the middle of the century its seaboard supported in some respects a single 'Scandinavian' community of fashion or culture. The extent of a Viking political presence in Wales is more problematic. There is no evidence for an equivalent to the Scandinavian kingdom of Dublin, but some leaders had strong Welsh connections, and they ruled in Anglesey and mainland Gwynedd for a period (such as Óláf in the early eleventh century).

The annals give little indication of the purpose of the Viking raids. Certainly portable wealth, supplies and slaves were taken, sanctuaries and relics desecrated, and in 998 the Bishop of St David's, Morgeneu, was killed. An important objective of the later raids was probably the taking of captives, such as ruling persons and men of learning, for ransom: in one sense, a form of tribute-taking. For example, in 989 Maredudd ab Owain, great great grandson of Rhodri Mawr and king of Dyfed, was compelled to redeem captive Welshmen from slavery at a penny a head paid to *black gentiles*. During the late tenth and early eleventh centuries Æthelræd of England paid huge sums of tribute to Viking leaders, who extorted this in order to pay their armies for support in their power struggles. Payment to mercenaries was often in slaves, as paid to Norse and Irish mercenaries by Rhys ap Tewdwr, for help in reinstating him as ruler of Deheubarth *c.* 1088.

The sons of Harald, Magnús Haraldsson and Guthröth, were ousted from Lincoln in about 967 and became involved in the politics of Gwynedd in the 970s while based on the Isle of Man. They made efforts to gain political control of Anglesey, which they raided in 971, 980 and 987. King Edgar's circumnavigation of Wales to Chester appears to have impressed Magnús, who joined the ceremony of submission to him on the River Dee in 973 or 974. According to the Welsh annals, Guthröth joined forces with *black gentiles* to attack Anglesey in 987, and the raid was recorded in the Irish Annals of Ulster 'the battle of Manu [was won] by Aralt's son and the Danes, and a thousand were slain there'. According to the annals, Guthröth seized as many as 2000 men (slaves) from Anglesey. One source records that Magnús (*Maccus*) occupied the island, part of Iago's kingdom. This Scandinavian dominance was relatively short lived, for within 70 years the political situation had changed again. By 1039, Gruffudd ap Llywelyn had gained control of the Scandinavians in Wales and ruled as king of Gwynedd, and any claims of overlordship by Dublin ceased. From 1055 until his death in 1063, his rule extended notionally to all of Wales.

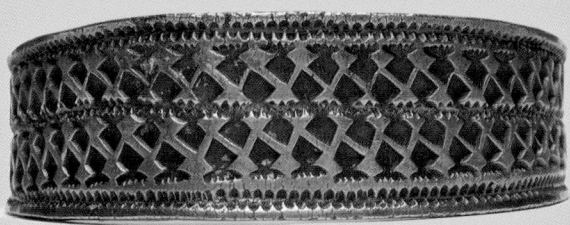

56 *One of five silver arm-rings of Hiberno-Norse type from Red Wharf Bay, Anglesey. They are similar in date to the great Cuerdale hoard from the River Ribble near Preston, buried about 905, shortly after Viking leader Ingimund's expulsion from Anglesey. (NMW 28.215)*

Cnut

The rule of the greatest of Viking kings, Cnut (ruled 1016-35) was to extend to some of north Wales. In 1014 Svein Forkbeard, the ruler of Denmark who had launched huge raids on England, died while on campaign there. The Danish fleet, together with the English leaders of the kingdom of Lindsey chose his son, Cnut, as leader. Cnut was forced initially to withdraw to Denmark, but returned in 1015 with a fleet of 200 ships. He took control of the kingdom of Northumbria in 1016 and fought a series of brutal engagements with Æthelræd's son, Edmund Ironside. At the battle of Ashingdon in Essex in October of that year, he defeated Edmund, and in November they decided to share the kingdom between them – Cnut gaining Mercia and the Danelaw. On Edmund's death shortly afterwards, Cnut became king of all England, which at that time included land that was to become Flintshire (*Tegeingl*). He was one of the strongest Viking kings, a firm ruler of England who continued a policy of heavy and unpopular taxation, introduced by Æthelræd, called *heregeld* to support a mercenary army and fleet. During his reign, there was a lull in the annalistic record of Viking raiding, though St David's suffered in 1022.

57 *Silver penny of Cnut (1016-35) of 'pointed helmet'-type from the hoard of 204 coins found at Bryn Maelgwyn, Gwynedd. It was struck by the Shrewsbury mint. The hoard was buried c. 1024. (NMW 79.105H/202)*

58 *Cnut and his queen, Emma (Aelfgifu) depicted presenting a cross at New Minster, Winchester, from the contemporary* Liber Vitae *of Hyde Abbey. Cnut sought acceptance by contemporaries and courted the church as an important instrument of reconciliation. Note the shape of the sword pommel and the style of dress. (London, British Library, Stowe 944, fol. 6r. By permission of The British Library)*

The Later Raids

Following a relatively peaceful period, a third phase of raiding commenced during the second half of the eleventh century, linked to events leading up to the Norman Conquest of Wales. From the late tenth century, Scandinavian presence grew in the Severn Estuary, Bristol replacing Chester as the main focus for Hiberno-Norse trading contact with Anglo-Saxon England. Following the plundering of Glamorgan by Count Eilaf (1018-24), a Dane in the service of King Cnut, the clergy fled from Llancarfan with relics and the shrine of the saint. According to the *Life of St Cadog*, the Danes and English attacked them at Mamhilad (*Mammeliat*) near Usk in Monmouthshire, one attacker succeeding in cutting off a 'gilded wing' (finial) of the shrine with his axe. Gruffudd ap Llywelyn, king of Gwynedd (1039-63) extended his rule to the eastern reaches of the Bristol Channel (the kingdoms of Morgannwg and Gwent). Making use of both rivalries in England during the reign of Edward the Confessor and the actions of Vikings, Gruffudd eventually ruled the whole of what is now known as Wales and owned his own fleet. He became renowned as a war-leader who, according to the *Chronicle of the Princes*, 'hounded the pagans and Saxons in many battles'.

60 *Map of later Viking raids. The pattern of raiding was linked to Viking fortunes in Ireland – increasing when events were unfavourable there, and slowing in Wales by the mid-1050s. Problems closer to home overshadowed the Hiberno-Norse threat.*

59 *Maredudd ap Edwin (died 1035) restored the line of Rhodri to the throne of Deheubarth in 1033. He has been identified with the 'Margiteut' commemorated in the inscription on the cross at Carew, Pembrokeshire. ECMW 303.*

To some during the eleventh century, the Scandinavians were allies and a source of mercenaries, and it was a period of alliance between Gwynedd and the Norse rulers of Dublin and Man. Professor Wendy Davies has even

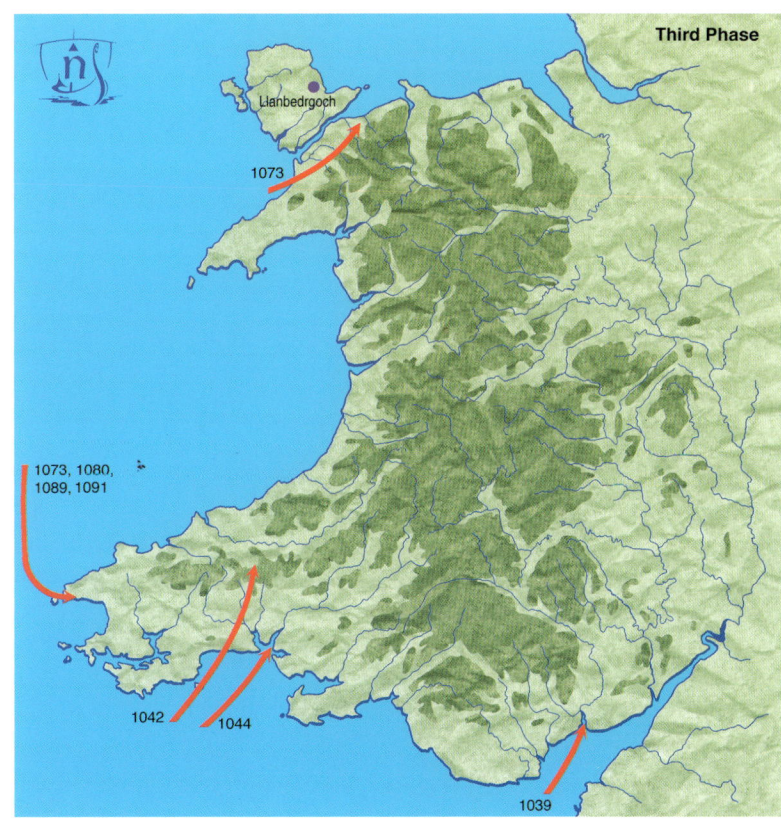

The Battle of the Menai Straits

The Norwegian king Magnús Barelegs (*Magnús berfœttr*) led a brutal campaign to extend his authority over Man and the Isles in 1098, which was also to bring to an end the Norman foothold on Anglesey and Arfon, which had been established *c.* 1090. In an effort to resist the Normans under Hugh de Montgomery (Earl of Shrewsbury) and Hugh of Chester, King Cadwgan ap Bleddyn of Powys joined forces on Anglesey with Gruffudd ap Cynan, who had gained the support of sixteen ships from Muirchertach Uí Briain, Irish king of Munster. Unfortunately, these ships defected to the Normans, and Gruffudd fled back to Ireland with his ally and son-in-law, Cadwgan ap Bleddyn. Providentially, a few days later Magnús' fleet arrived unexpectedly off Anglesey (in 'Öngul-sound') on the side of the Welsh and approached the island with three ships. A combined Welsh and Norwegian force defeated the Normans in battle, during which the Earl of Shrewsbury ('Hugh the Valiant') was killed (reputedly being shot in the eye by Magnús himself). The event was celebrated by the court poet Thorkel hamarskáld

'Arrow drummed on mail-coat. The chieftain shot forcefully. The mighty ruler of the people of Agder bent his bow. Blood sprayed on helmets. Bowstring-hail [arrows] flew into ring-mail, the troop fell, and the prince of the people of Hordaland caused the earl to be slain in a hard fight for land.'
(translation by Judith Jesch)

This victory at the battle of the Menai Straits enabled Gruffudd ap Cynan to return to Anglesey and consolidate his hold upon Gwynedd, which by 1114 he securely ruled. In 1103 Magnús visited Anglesey to obtain timber for the construction of fortifications on Man.

61 *Copper alloy sword pommels of late lobed form typical of the tenth or eleventh century, from Llan-faes, Anglesey and a site near Pembroke, Milford Haven. Welsh, Anglo–Saxon or Viking warriors could have used them. Left: width 51.1mm. (NMW 96.17H). Right: width 42mm.*

suggested a degree of Scandinavian rule in north Wales by the early eleventh century. Gruffudd ap Llywelyn sacked Hereford in 1055 with the help of Leofric of Mercia's son, the outlawed and banished Earl Ælfgar, and eighteen Norse ships from Ireland. To seal this new alliance, he married Ælfgar's daughter, Ealdgyth. Gruffudd was murdered in 1063 after a series of crushing defeats at the hands of Harold Godwinesson and his brother Tostig. Harold married Gruffudd ap Llywelyn's widow Ealdgyth, only to meet his death a few years later at the hands of William of Normandy at Hastings in 1066.

Gruffudd ap Cynan (1055-1137) was born in Dublin of mixed Welsh-Ostman-Irish ancestry and grew up among the Danish community in Dublin. He made several attempts to re-establish the old line of Rhodri as ruler of Gwynedd in the later eleventh century. After one failure, he stayed with the king

62 *St Peter of York silver penny from the 1894 Bangor hoard, with sword emblem (minted c. 910–19). (University of Wales Collection, Bangor Museum & Art Gallery 790)*

63 *Coin of Sigtrygg silkbeard, Sigtryggr Ólafsson, 'Silkiskeggi' (989-1036), King of the Irish [+ SITERIC REX IRVM], from the Bryn Maelgwyn hoard, Gwynedd. According to* the Historia Gruffud vab Kenan, *his son Ólaf Sihtricsson settled in Gwynedd, building a strong castle called 'the castle of king Ólaf or in Welsh 'Bon y Dom'. (NMW 79.105H/204)*

of Dublin (Diarmait Uí Briain) while he gathered assistance for his next expedition to Wales. The king presented him with a fleet manned by Danes, Irishmen and Britons. In 1081 he joined up with Rhys ap Tewdwr, who was claiming kingship of Deheubarth, and together they defeated three native princelings, Trahaearn ap Caradog (ruler of Arwystli and later Gwynedd), Meilyr ap Rhiwallon and Caradog ap Gruffudd (ruler of Morgannwg) at the battle of Mynydd Carn near Fishguard.

It is hardly surprising that Norse and Hiberno-Norse fleets were a prominent component of Welsh politics. However, not all expeditions were successful. On one occasion (c. 1087?), Gruffudd ap Cynan led a raid of twenty-four ships up the Severn Estuary. According to the *Life of St Gwynllyw* compiled about 1130, disaster struck during their return from Barry ad Orcades (to the Orkney Islands, used as a place of refuge), following their desecration of the church of St Gwynllyw (now known as St Woolos' Cathedral, Newport): '...The ships were under canvas, but the sails could not face the winds for their raging violence. The more the rowers rowed in one direction, by so much the more did the billows thrust them back athwart. The

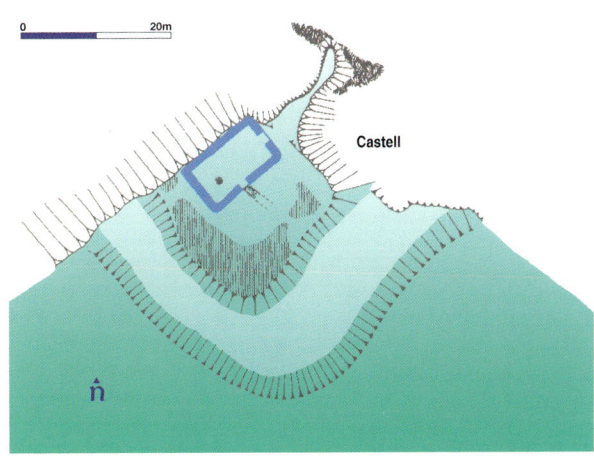

64 *The small coastal promontory fort at Castell, Porth Trefadog, Anglesey, has been associated with the eleventh- to twelfth-century links between the kings of Gwynedd and the Vikings of Dublin and Man. (Courtesy of the Gwynedd Archaeological Trust)*

ship's gear, shaking, became shattered' (*Vita Sancti Gundleii*, ch.12; translation by A.W. Wade-Evans). The whole fleet, with the exception of two boats, was sunk before it could reach the shore.

65 *Priestholm* (presta-
holmr), *also known as
Puffin Island or Ynys
Seiriol, Anglesey. In the
background lies Penmon.
(Crown copyright: Royal
Commission on the
Ancient and Historical
Monuments of Wales)*

The Viking Warrior

All Norse freemen were entitled to carry weapons and expected to assemble when directed to do so by their king or overlord. The Vikings generally fought on foot, their main weapons being the spear, battle-axe or sword. Bows and single-edged long knives, called saxes, have also been found in the graves which contained the weapons and equipment of fighting men. The type of weapon and its quality would have reflected the status of the person buried.

The sword was the finest of their weapons, prized both for hand-to-hand fighting and as a symbol of aristocratic power. The commonest form was the broad, straight two-edged blade, usually about a metre long. An elaborately decorated hilt would reflect the high rank of a noble warrior. Many Viking swords have been found either in graves or in rivers. Sword pommels were usually of iron, but examples made of copper alloy have been found. One exceptionally fine brass Viking sword hilt was found in 1992 in the sea about sixteen miles (26 km) off the coast of Pembrokeshire, on the Smalls Reef. Its double-edged blade, the most important part of the sword, had not survived, but it may have been pattern-welded to provide both strength and an exotic appearance.

66 Iron spearhead and broad-bladed axe from Insula XII, Caerwent. The axe has a curving edge and concave sided blade (length 132 mm), and part of the axe shaft has been preserved. Both weapons may be late ninth or tenth century in date. In the eulogy to Gruffudd ap Cynan, special tribute is paid to 'The men of Denmark with their two-edged axes' (ac eu bwyeill deuvinyauc) at the battle of Mynydd Carn (1081). Spear: length 550mm. (Newport Museum & Art Gallery; NPTMG: D2/43). Axe: width 126mm. (Newport Museum & Art Gallery; NPTMG: D2/904)

67 A fine pendant whetstone found within the enclosure at Llanbedrgoch, Anglesey provides a clue to the warrior status of some people. The silvered bronze ferrule, which takes the form of a pointed helmet with nose guard when viewed from any side, has a suspension ring so that the whetstone could hang from a belt. It probably served both to sharpen a fine sword blade and to act as a symbol of power and authority. The sharpening and polishing of a blade was a skilled task, as indicated in the Welsh Mabinogion, when Wrnach the Giant seeks someone to polish his sword. A 'sword sharpener', swurd hwita, was among the officers in the household of Prince Æthelstan of Wessex in the eleventh century. Overall length 267mm. (NMW 95.46H/1)

Axes took several forms according to function – whether for working wood, hunting or fighting. By the eleventh century, specialised broad-bladed axes had developed to be wielded by two hands. On the Bayeux Tapestry, they appear as a distinctive weapon in Harold's army. Archers armed with bows and arrows also formed part of a warrior band, their actions being praised in poetic celebrations of battles (such as the battle of the Menai Straits in 1098).

Very few Viking helmets have been discovered, but representations in miniature are found, as well as on coins. They can be seen on some of the chessmen from the great hoard of twelfth-century ivory and whalebone chess pieces discovered in 1831 on the Isle of Lewis, Outer Hebrides. Another depiction of a warrior's head, carved in antler, from Sigtuna, Sweden, shows a conical helmet with splayed nose guard, which is decorated with ring-and-dots. This motif forms a horizontal border and four vertical lines on the helmet. Ring-and-dot also decorates the nose guard of a helmet-shaped ferrule on a large whetstone from Llanbedrgoch, Anglesey (see figure 67). Such equipment probably belonged to rich and powerful warriors, and is unlikely to have belonged to the common fighting man, farmer or fisherman.

Spears are among the most common weapons found in graves. While some were pattern-welded or highly decorated, many were cheaper to manufacture, needing little iron. In addition to their use for hunting, spears were the only effective thrusting weapons available, which kept an assailant at long range in hand-to-hand combat. One such socketed spearhead measuring '20 inches' (about 50cm) in length was found in a Viking grave at Talacre, Flintshire, in the 1930s, while another found with an axe at Caerwent, Monmouthshire, may also have been placed in a grave (though nothing was recorded of their precise relationship when they were discovered in 1910 or 1911).

The Vikings protected themselves in battle with circular shields covering the body from shoulder to thigh. These were made of wood (such as lime) and sometimes bound in leather and metal bindings; they could be decorated with metal mounts, and an iron boss in the centre protected the carrying hand. By the eleventh century, kite-shaped shields had grown in popularity.

68 *Iron stirrups from St Mary Hill, Glamorgan. Each stirrup has a square loop continuous with the bowed arms, folded to form a deep tread. Late ninth or tenth century. Heights 232mm and 233mm. (NMW 94.250)*

Mounted warriors were less common, though represented by the occasional burial of horses with rich Vikings, and the discovery of riding equipment. One of only three pairs of Viking stirrups from Britain and the Isle of Man was found in Wales during the nineteenth century at St Mary Hill, Glamorgan. Their features suggest that they probably come from a pagan Viking burial of the late ninth or tenth century.

It is easy to overemphasise the difference between the equipment used by Viking and native warriors, for similar gear will have been available to both sides. However, the strategy of each may have differed.

69 *Chain mail garments were sometimes worn by warriors. This set of reproduction equipment is shown being worn at Llanbedrgoch, Anglesey.*

The Smalls Reef Sword Guard

This brass sword guard is ornamented on both sides with a pair of stylised animals in profile, interwoven with a pair of thin snake-like beasts in a fluent version of the late Viking artistic style known as *Urnes*. Inlaid strips of silver wire have been used to highlight and embellish the design,

70 *The Smalls Reef Sword Guard.*

while the cross-hatching acted as a base for an applied black niello, which would have created a dramatic contrasting background. On the top of the guard, two small beasts in Irish style bite both sides of the hilt.

The guard is dated stylistically to about 1100-25, and relates to metalwork and woodwork produced in Ireland during the eleventh century. The strong symmetry and diagonal composition of the design is reminiscent of the decoration on Irish ecclesiastical metalwork of the period, and local influence is evident in the details of the beasts. The technical brilliance of the guard reflects the level of prestige reached by secular patronage in early twelfth-century Ireland. Width 118mm. (NMW 92.57H)

Masters of Wide Seas

'Bitter is the wind tonight
It tosses the ocean's white tresses;
I do not fear the wild warriors of Norway
Sailing on the Irish Sea.'

(Irish stanza, St Gall Lib., ninth century; translation by K.H. Jackson, 1935)

The capability to build full ocean-going ships – evoked as 'iron-studded dragons', 'sea steeds' and 'well-carved hulls' – made possible the movement of Vikings across the North Sea, the Irish Sea and the North Atlantic. The distinctive double-ended form of the square-rigged, single-masted Viking ship with rising bow and stern represents the perfection of a ship design within a Northern European tradition of shipbuilding which goes back at least to the fifth century AD. In time, regional and functional differences in boat type developed, which were important for Viking life, whether to harvest the sea or travel. By the eleventh century, there were small coastal traders, broad cargo carriers and large swift warships up to 35m in length, as well as tiny two-rower *faerings* ('four-oared'). The fleets could vary in size from a dozen or so to several hundred, though some of the larger figures quoted in the sagas may have been exaggerated. Despite sailing skills transmitted through the generations, and methods of navigation with and without landmarks, Viking seafarers were still vulnerable to being blown off course and driven onto rocks. The *Chronicle of the Princes* records that in the year 1050 or 1052 a fleet from Ireland foundered off the Welsh kingdom of Deheubarth ('the south parts'), and illustrates the size of some calamities.

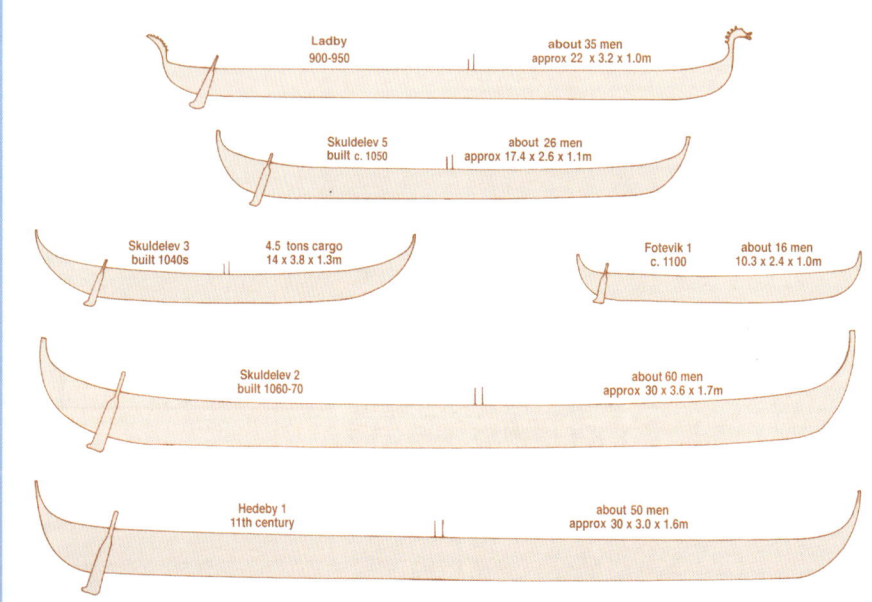

71 *Silhouettes of various boats, showing the range of sizes and capacities. (Based on O. Crumlin-Pedersen 1991)*

Ladby
900-950
about 35 men
approx 22 x 3.2 x 1.0m

Skuldelev 5
built c. 1050
about 26 men
approx 17.4 x 2.6 x 1.1m

Skuldelev 3
built 1040s
4.5 tons cargo
14 x 3.8 x 1.3m

Fotevik 1
c. 1100
about 16 men
10.3 x 2.4 x 1.0m

Skuldelev 2
built 1060-70
about 60 men
approx 30 x 3.6 x 1.7m

Hedeby 1
11th century
about 50 men
approx 30 x 3.0 x 1.6m

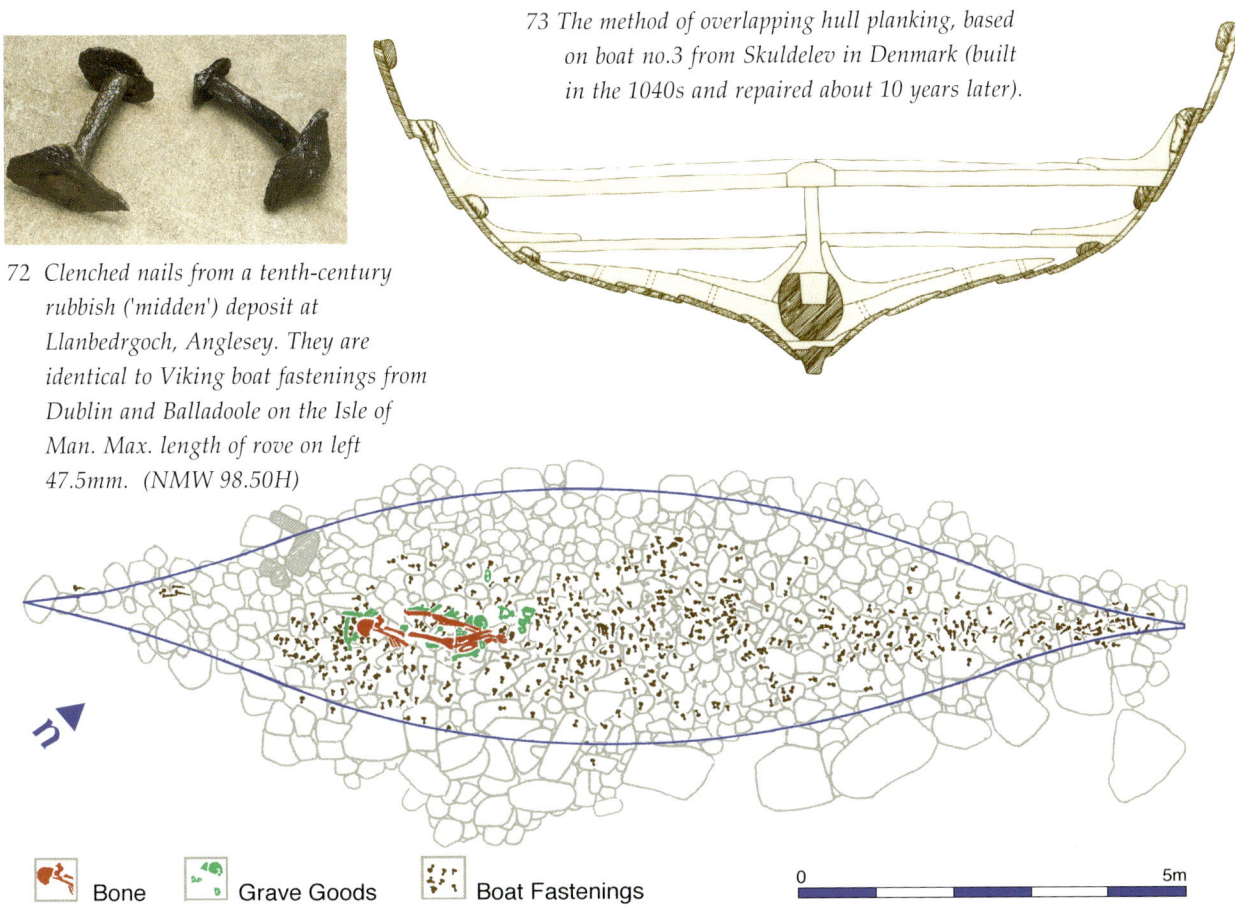

72 Clenched nails from a tenth-century rubbish ('midden') deposit at Llanbedrgoch, Anglesey. They are identical to Viking boat fastenings from Dublin and Balladoole on the Isle of Man. Max. length of rove on left 47.5mm. (NMW 98.50H)

73 The method of overlapping hull planking, based on boat no.3 from Skuldelev in Denmark (built in the 1040s and repaired about 10 years later).

Bone Grave Goods Boat Fastenings

0 5m

74 The early tenth-century Viking boat-burial at Balladoole, Isle of Man. Though disturbed, the position of the clenched nails, skeleton and grave goods suggest a general layout for both boat and burial. The warrior was buried with weapons and equipment (bridle, stirrups and spurs) and wore an Irish ringed pin to fasten the cloak. A female body was also buried, without grave-goods.

Boats were expensive to build. Several thousand clenched nails (several hundred kilos of iron) were needed to fasten the overlapping hull planks (in 'clinker' fashion) of a modest 14m long boat. Floor timbers (the lower ribs) were fastened to the planking, but not directly to the keel, producing a flexible hull with excellent seafaring characteristics. The shallow draught of the vessels gave them the capability of travelling up rivers and beaching on shelving shores without need of quays.

Archaeological evidence for Viking boats in the Britain and Ireland is largely limited to boat timbers which have been re-used within waterfront structures and a few ninth- or tenth-century boat graves in Scotland (such as Scar on Sanday in Orkney) and on the Isle of Man (such as Balladoole).

The Smalls Reef Viking shipwreck

About seven nautical miles (13 km) due west of the island of Grassholm in the Irish Sea lie hazardous, partially exposed tips of basalt and dolerite formations, known today as *The Smalls*. In 1991, a sports diver spotted a bluish object protruding from beneath one of the metal plates from one of the modern shipwrecks, which litter the seabed around these rocks and gullies. The object later proved to be a late Viking brass sword guard (see p. 55).

The reef was investigated during an expedition organised by the National Museum of Wales in 1992 in order to record in detail the find-spot and assess the likelihood of further Viking Age material being preserved. There was little chance of large sections of boat structure surviving in such an unyielding, hostile environment, but small objects may have become buried, lodged between rocks or embedded in concretion. The search involved difficult diving between tides in the narrow, steep-sided rock gullies around the nineteenth-century lighthouse, usually while a swell rolled unhindered from the Atlantic to break against the rocks.

75 above, 76 below. South-west Wales and the location of the Smalls Reef.

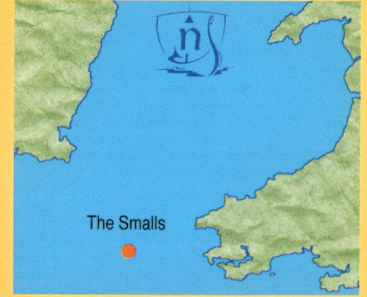

The sword guard had been discovered at the end of one of the gullies, in about 11m of water. It had been trapped beneath a large iron plate thought to come from the broken hull of the steam ship *Rhiwabon*, wrecked on the same spot in 1884. No trace of the rest of the sword has yet been found, and the guard may have been separated from the other components by later events, such as the loss of the *Rhiwabon*, whose lower hull has now concreted to the rock.

Such a valuable weapon, perhaps a personal possession or gift to a friend or ally, would probably have been wrapped in a watertight leather bag or safely stowed on board in a chest. The boat on which it was carried came to grief on The Smalls, along one of the long-distance sea routes, at some time during the early twelfth century - a period of frequent contact between Wales and Ireland. An area 200m in diameter around the presumed site of the scattered wreck is now scheduled under the *Protection of Wrecks Act 1973*.

77 *The quest for evidence for a wreck depended largely on the endurance of the diving team (some shown here entering the water during the 1992 expedition) and what could be achieved by direct observation.*

78 *Further evidence of a Viking period boat may lie sealed beneath these iron plates from the hull of the SS Rhiwabon (wrecked on these rocks in 1884).*

79 *The finder of the sword guard prepares to dive, with the Smalls in the background.*

The Newport Boat

In 1877, workmen came across a portion of the side of an ancient boat during the course of excavating a new timber pond for the Alexandra Dock, between the mouths of the Rivers Usk and Ebbw at Newport. The fragment of oak planking, which overlapped in clinker fashion and was fastened by iron clenched nails, had been retained in an upright position by sharpened oak stakes. The antiquary Octavius Morgan considered that is was most probably a vessel which formed part of the Danish fleets which invaded that part of the country in early periods. He based this conclusion on the method of construction, the dockmaster's opinion that *Dantzig oak* from the Baltic had been used and a belief that the guessed date ('about AD 900') correlated with the chronicle entries. By comparison with recent finds elsewhere, however, it is now evident that the Newport boat was a salvaged section of hull re-used within a waterfront revetment or similar type of structure. Radiocarbon dating of the one surviving section of boat planking has provided a date for the sample of *c.* 920-1080. The position of the sample within the inner growth rings of the tree suggests that the boat may have been built as much as 80 years later than the sample date.

80 The surviving section of hull planking found in 1877 at Newport. Maximum plank width 156mm. (Newport Museum & Art Gallery; NPTMG: 30.54)

To judge from the waterlogged ship timbers found in Viking Dublin, Norse craft influenced shipwrights in those lands they reached. One of the Skuldelev longships found at Roskilde Fjord in Denmark was built of oak from the Irish Sea region, perhaps from forests around Dublin. Similar ships were certainly used by the later Welsh princes, who recognised the importance of naval power. In the *Anglo-Saxon Chronicle's* account of Earl Harold's attack on Rhuddlan, the Saxon forces burnt Gruffudd ap Llywelyn's boats and sails. On Gruffudd's murder in August 1063, his head was delivered to Harold who brought it to King Edward the Confessor 'together with the figure-head of his ship and the adornments with it' (boat figure-heads were removable).

Mobility was certainly of great strategic and economic advantage, and the freedom of action was dependent on maritime ability. The Scandinavian names for navigation points around Wales illustrate the effective opening up of trading routes, as a continuous process of their merchant endeavour.

Traders

Commerce was important to the Vikings, and many Scandinavians were merchants rather than pirates. Many would also have been part-time farmers and some will have engaged in craft activities. Initially high value goods would have been acquired as plunder or tribute (huge quantities of silver were paid as *gafol* from England and the Continent). Much trade would have been coastal in character and local, covering short distances. A small number of trading centres such as Ribe in Denmark grew up from seasonal meeting places which attracted merchants from far afield, some of which developed into towns. By the tenth century, the Viking trade network stretched from Iceland to the Caspian Sea, and was responsible for introducing large quantities of silver from the Middle East into Europe, in exchange for furs, hides, perishables, cloth, weapons and slaves. Trade in western Britain revolved around the Irish Sea, and commodities probably included slaves, wheat, woollens, horses, tin, copper and silver.

81 Isolated finds are occasionally made, such as these decorated merchants' lead weights from the beach at Freshwater West (bottom) and a site near Milford Haven (top), both in Pembrokeshire. Bottom: weight 238.9g, length 54mm. (Bottom: NMW 30.110; top: NMW 92.12H)

During the late ninth and first half of the tenth centuries, Wales, Scotland and Ireland lacked a tradition of minting, and coins were only struck in Ireland from *c.* 995. In their homelands, the Vikings

82 A selection of the lead weights of diverse form and size which have been found at Llanbedrgoch, Anglesey. Two are capped with recycled ninth-century Insular metalwork (an enamelled mount and gilt bronze terminal from a ninth-century pseudo-penannular brooch). A number are close in weight to the basic unit of weight found at Viking Dublin (26.6g, close to the Roman and Carolingian ounce). (NMW 95.5H/96.41H/98.50H)

83 *The hoard of silver found on the High St, Bangor (within the ancient monastic precinct), was deposited after c. 925. It is thought to be characteristically Scandinavian in coin composition, and may have been hidden by a merchant or trader. It contains Arabic silver (Kufic) dirhems, Anglo-Saxon and Viking Kingdom of York coins, a fragment of arm-ring and a fragment of silver ingot (both hack-silver). A second, later, hoard from Bangor comprises a small group of coins deposited c. 970, also in the vicinity of the monastery established by St Deiniol in the sixth century. (University of Wales Collection, Bangor Museum & Art Gallery 790)*

and during the ninth century the pattern suggests that Carolingian coins minted in western France, in particular Melle, south-west of Poitiers, were reaching Ireland and Wales direct (as illustrated by the hoards from Mullaghbogen, Co. Kildare, Minchin Hole on the Gower and Llanbedrgoch). The first half of the tenth century witnessed a peak of burying large hoards, and the distribution of known Viking silver hoards in Wales is entirely coastal in character. Those in Wales are unlikely to be plunder from churches, but rather the import of silver into Wales and an index of Scandinavian activity, while others may have been buried by native hands. The later coin hoard buried at Bryn Maelgwyn near Llandudno was deposited in the mid-1020s and may be Viking booty rather than local savings. A shadowy 'find' from Rhos Fawr, Llandyfrydog, Anglesey, is said to have included a silver penny of Edgar (959-75).

The hoard of five pristine silver Hiberno-Norse arm-rings from the Tan Dinas quarry on the south-eastern side of Red Wharf Bay, Anglesey, and the Cuerdale hoard (some 40kg of silver buried on the banks of the River Ribble about 905) have both been associated with events surrounding the expulsion of Ingimund and his fellow Vikings from Dublin and then Anglesey.

did not issue coins as currency. Instead, they used silver and occasionally gold for trading either in ingot form or as 'hack-silver' (silver ornaments, jewellery or ingots which had been cut up) for exchange by weight. Coins, many removed from their normal area of circulation, were also used as bullion. The flow of silver is reflected by the composition and location of Viking silver hoards, which sometimes contain a mixture of coins and hack-silver gathered through plunder, tribute or transaction.

The evidence of coin loss suggests an emergent trade between the Irish coastline and north-west Mercia from the first quarter of the eighth century,

84   *Lead weights and folding scales with pans suspended on chains were used to weigh silver coins.*

85   *Some of the silver and bronze objects found at
Llanbedrgoch, Anglesey, provide a clear link to the
Viking world. These silver ingots and fragments of
arm-ring of tenth-century date bear shear marks
which indicate that the armlets have been used as
'hack-silver' bullion for trading. Arm-ring widths
21mm and 22.5mm. Ingot lengths 18.4mm,
17.25mm. (NMW 95.46H/96.41H)*

- ▲ More than 5 finds of Chesterware
- ▲ Less than 5 finds of Chesterware
- ▼ Kiln site

86 Trade networks may be indicated by certain artefact types from recognisable sources. The distribution of wheel-thrown pottery produced in Stafford and possibly elsewhere in the north-west Midlands provides one such clue. It is known as 'Chester ware' after the first example to be recognised, the container for the Castle Esplanade hoard dated c. 970 . Long since recognised at a number of sites in the West Midlands, small quantities of Chester ware have now been found at Rhuddlan and Llanbedrgoch in north Wales, Monmouth and Viking Dublin. However, to judge from its rarity few people in Wales used pottery at this time, and vessels of wood or leather would have been commonplace.
(Based on maps by P.H. Alebon, Grosvenor Museum, Chester, and D. Ford, The Potteries Museum & Art Gallery, Stoke-on-Trent)

Meols

An important trading centre once existed at Meols (like Milford, from Old Norse *melr*, 'sandbank') near the mouth of the Dee on the Wirral Peninsula. Artefacts such as ringed pins and Scandinavian-style metalwork from the site indicate that it had an important role in Viking period trading. Recent work on coastal trading ports of the Irish Sea has illustrated the development of this trade. At Meols, metalwork of seventh- to ninth-century date appears to be increasingly dominated by Anglo-Saxon objects, and there is a good coin series which includes Byzantine coins, sceattas, stycas, over twenty-five late Saxon silver coins and one possible Hiberno-Norse penny. Scandinavian settlement in the Wirral about 905 and the establishment of a royal *burh* at Chester gave Meols a new lease of life as a trading port, and the great variety of metalwork among the tenth- and eleventh-century finds illustrates regular long-distance contact with traders from England, the Irish Sea region and beyond.

87 Stirrup strap-mount, originally for fastening a strap to an iron stirrup, from Meols. Crudely incised ribbon-like beast in Anglo-Scandinavian Ringerike style, within a four-sided frame and extension at the top. Height about 55mm. (Grosvenor Museum, Chester)

Breaking New Ground

The extent to which Viking people and their culture became integrated into native Welsh society is the subject of an investigation on the island of Anglesey. The excavation of an intriguing settlement complex of early medieval date at Llanbedrgoch may provide the key to unlock details of life in ninth- and tenth-century Wales.

In 1992, some metal detected finds were identified from several fields near Red Wharf Bay. These included a penny of Wulfred of Canterbury (struck 805-32), Carolingian deniers of Louis the Pious (struck 822-40) and Charles the Bald (struck 848-77) and lead weights of Viking type. An earlier isolated find of an Anglo-Saxon penny of Cynethryth, wife of King Offa (757-96), was reported from the vicinity in 1989. The finders were able to indicate the general find-spots, but there were no visible signs of a settlement in the form of humps or depressions.

The first task was to determine whether any evidence could be found for the original context of these finds. In 1994 a combination of geophysical surveying and trial excavation by a team from the National Museums & Galleries of Wales produced exciting results within a few days.

A magnetometer survey of the field which had produced the Viking weights indicated with unexpected clarity the presence of a buried ditch enclosing a large U-shaped area on a gentle slope facing south, in the direction of Red Wharf Bay. Limited excavation established that this ditch was rock-cut in parts and about 2m wide and 1m deep;

88 Geophysical surveying of one of the fields at Llanbedrgoch in 1994. The magnetometer, which measures very small variations in the earth's magnetic field caused by buried features, is carried along regularly spaced traverses within a series of 20m x 20m grids strung out on the ground. Readings are automatically recorded via a sample trigger, for downloading onto computer.

89 The prompt reporting of metal detected finds by Mr Archie Gillespie (shown here) and Mr Peter Corbett led to the discovery of the site at Llanbedrgoch.

Conservation and Discovery

When first found, this iron bridle mount from the site at Llanbedrgoch resembled a large plain nail head (a), but X-radiography of the corroded iron revealed a more complex shape (b), and careful laboratory cleaning uncovered this remarkable Irish enamelled mount (c-d). Conservation is an integral part of the quest for evidence from the past.

The cells are filled with either red or yellow enamel forming a stepped pattern around a central equal-armed cross. The use of iron for enamelwork in the medieval Celtic tradition is virtually unknown in contemporary Europe and rare in Ireland. A centrally placed, pierced lug on the reverse would originally have fastened it to a leather strap. Enamelled mounts of this type in copper alloy have been found on the Isle of Man, in Ireland and Norway, and most have been found in Viking Age burials with horse bridle fittings.

90 *Iron bridle mount,*
    Llanbedrgoch.
    Diameter 24.5mm.
    (NMW 98.50H)

a   *b*   *c*   *d*

91 *Excavation of trench R2 in 1998 uncovered a flagged surface for a ninth-century structure (foreground) and the*
    enclosure ditch (background).

a range of dates from the sixth to the eleventh centuries was obtained by radiocarbon dating of the charcoal in its fills. A second small excavation of a 'hot spot' of magnetic activity recorded by the survey within the enclosure uncovered a post-hole cut into a rock-cut platform, and this was thought to represent a house. Radiocarbon dates from charcoal found within the post-hole confirmed an eighth- to tenth-century date.

There have since been five main areas of excavation within the enclosure, and the complicated history of the site is becoming apparent with the assistance of radiocarbon and archaeomagnetic dating techniques, coupled to analysis of the stratigraphy and of particular object types.

92 A 'total station' theodolite with electronic distance measuring is used to record findspots and trench details.

93 Top right: site surveyor and illustrator David Stevens using a drawing frame to produce a stone-by-stone plan of the features found during the 1998 season

94 Finds processing during the excavation in 1995. The large quantities of animal bone and other artefacts are carefully labelled and catalogued.

95 Supervisor Mark Lodwick completes a record of a feature in trench H (1995), describing its shape, size, position and fill type.

96 *Students of
archaeology undertake
initial cleaning of a
massive enclosure
wall discovered in
1998.*

Llanbedrgoch: from Farm to Trading Centre

Some of the natural attractions of the site at Llanbedrgoch during the ninth and tenth centuries were evident at earlier periods. The site is situated on a carefully selected, sheltered location on a rise with a freshwater supply, about 1000m from the sea, astride a natural route from the sheltered haven of Red Wharf Bay. It is clear that a freshwater spring at the lower perimeter of the enclosure had been a focus of activity from as early as the Neolithic (c. 3300 BC), a period when most of the burial chambers on Anglesey are thought to have been built. A small number of artefacts and radiocarbon dates point to activity between the first and sixth centuries AD. By combining traditional archaeological dating methods of stratigraphy and typology with scientific techniques, it is now possible to subdivide the early medieval period on the site into a number of phases. A seventh-century native settlement developed into a tenth-century fortified settlement, which perhaps served as the hub of a larger group of open, undefended settlements.

During the first 'enclosed' phase, from about 600 (and possibly earlier), the main activity appears to have been farming. The wooden houses seem to have been built in the mixed tradition of circular round-houses and rectangular halls. At some point in the ninth century, the enclosure boundary was 'upgraded' into a defensive system with a solid dry-stone wall about 2.2m wide, sufficient for a wall walk. This substantial structure can be interpreted as an expression of power to deter potential raiders, coinciding with the period of initial Viking raids on North Wales.

97 Aerial view of Llanbedrgoch. The highlighted area indicates the extent of the fortified enclosure; about 1 ha. in area. (Crown Copyright; Royal Commission on the Ancient and Historical Monuments of Wales)

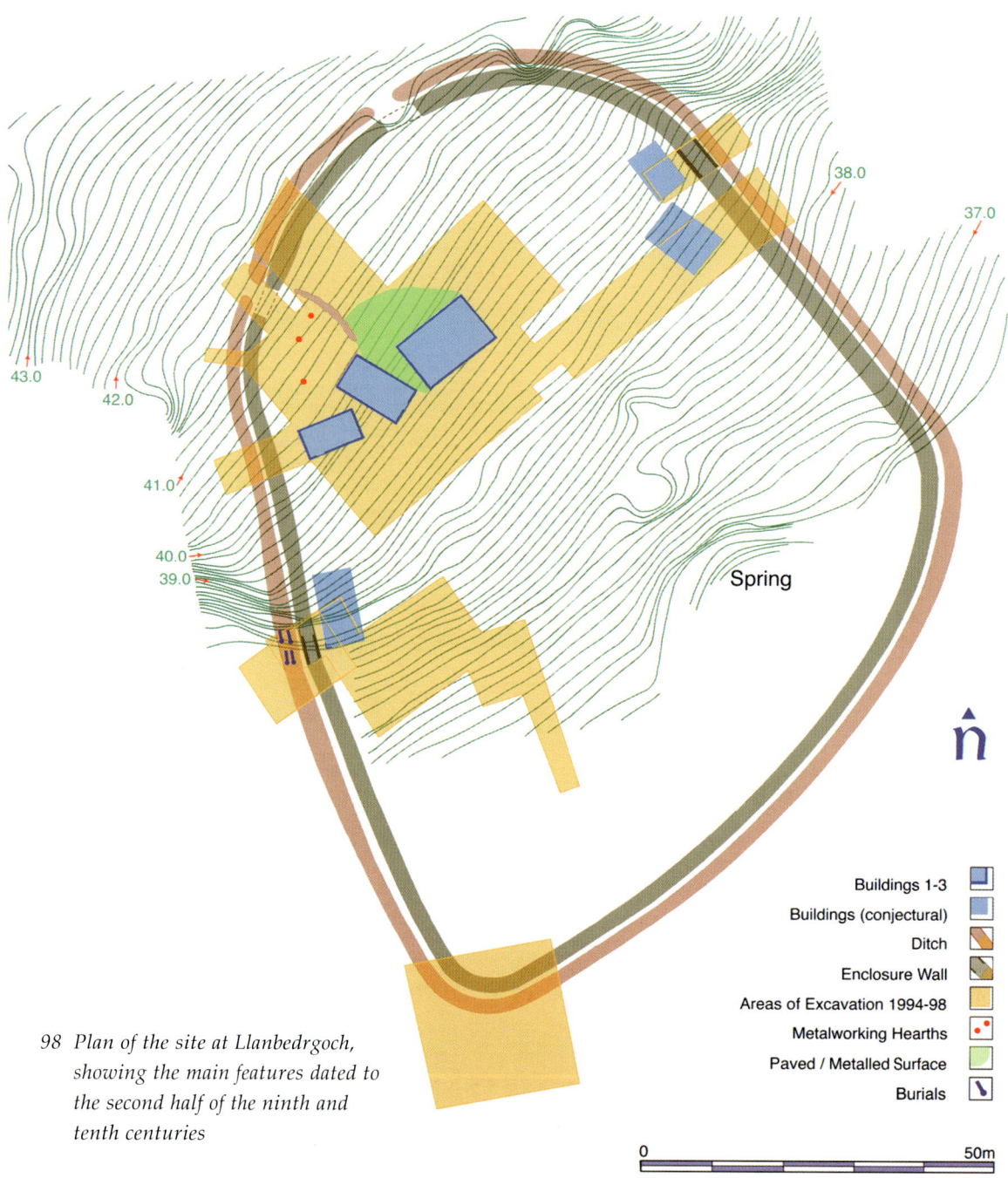

38.0

37.0

43.0

42.0

41.0

40.0
39.0

Spring

n̂

Buildings 1-3
Buildings (conjectural)
Ditch
Enclosure Wall
Areas of Excavation 1994-98
Metalworking Hearths
Paved / Metalled Surface
Burials

0   50m

98 *Plan of the site at Llanbedrgoch,
    showing the main features dated to
    the second half of the ninth and
    tenth centuries*

The role of Scandinavian settlers and traders is not straight forward, but some objects recovered from Llanbedrgoch bear the unmistakable mark of the Hiberno-Norse style typical of the Irish Sea area, such as hack-silver, merchants' weights, ringed pins and buckles. A rubbish dump in the south-west corner of the enclosure contained large quantities of animal bone, a range of artefacts and a copper alloy Northumbrian styca (penny) of Archbishop Wigmund (c. 848-58). There was at least one final structural phase within the enclosure, involving the construction of a large rectangular building, with a slightly raised central hearth. Layers within this building, which replaced Building 1, have provided a radiocarbon date of c. 785-1020. After this phase of occupation, the area appears to have reverted to agriculture, which together with stone robbing removed all obvious surface traces of the former settlement.

99 This fine seventh-century bird-headed brooch from Llanbedrgoch is paralleled by Anglian brooches from Yorkshire. It reminds us of pre-Viking contact between Anglesey and Northumbria. External diameter 28.5mm. (NMW 98.50H)

The excavation of the site has more than doubled the total number of Viking period artefacts previously known from Wales. They reveal clues as to the everyday function of the settlement, such as the working of leather (awls and socketed tools) and antler, the essential farming nature of the inhabitants (quernstones, grain, animal bone) and their trading activities (hack-silver, weights). These finds offer one means of assessing the degree to which Scandinavian culture was assimilated into the society of north Wales. They also suggest that the site attracted craftsmen and merchants as a component of Viking ('Hiberno-Norse') economic and political activity in the Irish Sea area.

100 The midden area in the south-west corner of the enclosure at Llanbedrgoch, under excavation in 1997. The accumulation of large quantities of rubbish at this point was intentional, helping to level the ground and stabilise an area which may have been prone to waterlogging.

A Mystery Unearthed

In August 1998, an unexpected and puzzling discovery was made at Llanbedrgoch. The skeletons of two individuals were found buried in the upper fill of a ditch situated immediately outside the defensive wall. Contrary to usual Christian practice, both skeletons were orientated north-south rather than east-west. The young adult was extended on its back, with slightly flexed legs; the younger skeleton of a child was crouched, lying on the left side. Both individuals appear to have died prematurely, and to have been buried at the same time beneath a rough pile of stones in this unusual location, rather than in the local cemetery. Had we at last come face to face with witnesses to the Viking period on Anglesey? Refinements in the technique of radiocarbon dating (called *Accelerator Mass*

102   *Recording burial 5 (adult) during the 1999 excavations.*

Spectrometry) now make it possible to date small samples of bone, and in November 1998 a sample was carefully taken from one of the leg bones of the extended burial. This high precision dating technique suggested that there was a 95% probability that death occurred between 770-970 (68% probability between 790-890). Charcoal recovered from the underlying ditch fill gave a radiocarbon date of *c.* 620-775, indicating that the ditch was silting up during the preceding century.

101   *Burials 1 (young adult) and 2 (child, in the far corner of the trench), as they first appeared in 1998.*

Excavations in 1999 established that at least three more individuals had been buried near by, without care or ceremony. Once again, their orientation was north-south rather than east-west. A young adolescent was found in the upper ditch fill, orientated with head to south and feet to north. An adult had been thrown directly on top of this adolescent, this time with head to north. To judge from the unusual positions of the arms, the adult's wrists may have been tied behind the back.

All the bodies appear to have been placed in shallow graves which probably utilised the depression caused by the silted up enclosure ditch. The circumstances of burial and lack of Christian orientation have led to speculation that they were victims of Viking raiding. All five individuals may have been interred at the same time, and no attempt appears to have been made to commemorate them or mark the location of their graves. This suggests that they had not been buried by their nearest of kin – but why not? A number of lines of inquiry are being pursued in order to establish age and cause of death, the probable date of death and whether any family links can be proven. Were they the unfortunate victims of violence? If so, who were the perpetrators? Vikings were not the only aggressors during this period, for Mercians destroyed Degannwy in 823 and were campaigning in north Wales for much of the ninth century (English killed Rhodri Mawr in 878). Nevertheless, in view of Llanbedrgoch's prominent location, Viking attack and take-over of the site, albeit for a short period, are distinct possibilities.

103   Burials 3 (adult), 4 (young adolescent) and 5 (adult), outside the defensive wall, displayed signs of casual and rapid burial.

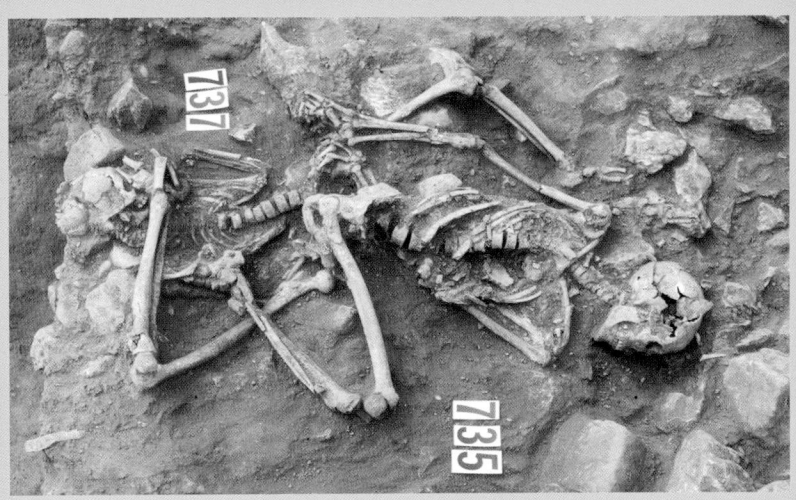

104   Burials 3 (735) and 4 (737), as excavated in 1999.

105 Reconstruction of the enclosure at Llanbedrgoch in the early tenth century, from the south. The interior appears to have been well organised, with ditched divisions, but the complete layout is not yet known. The huge enclosure wall at Llanbedrgoch reflects the prosperity of the owner and may have been constructed in the time of Rhodri Mawr (844-78) or his sons in response to Viking pressure.

106 The enclosure ditch at Llanbedrgoch was cut in the seventh century, if not earlier, and recut on at least two occasions

The settlement would appear to represent a new type of site for ninth and tenth-century Wales – a low-lying, fortified multifunctional centre. Several stages of Viking contact may be suggested.

Stage 1. Refortification of a low-lying coastal settlement in response to hostile Viking pressure during the ninth century.

Stage 2. The development of the site's potential as a trading post and multifunctional centre during the late ninth and early tenth centuries with the opening up of maritime commerce. Possibility of Viking raids and temporary take-over.

Stage 3. The integration of Sandinavians and native Welsh, and possibly even Norse residence.

Many questions about the site remain to be answered, such as:

Could it have been engaged in the collection of tolls and dues?

Who buried the bodies in the ditch fill, and why?

If there was a Viking take-over for some period, how long did it last ?

How densely populated was the enclosure during this period?

How did the site function within the precursor to the eleventh-century administrative system in north Wales?

Why did the site fail to develop in the twelfth century?

Where does its successor lie?

House and Home

There are difficulties in identifying specifically Scandinavian forms of building in rural Britain, and it has been assumed that many Viking period farms may lie beneath more recent farm complexes. In some areas halls with bow-sided walls have been linked with Viking presence, but some of these may have been constructed by native landowners influenced by Scandinavian building practice. At Ribblehead in the Pennines of north Yorkshire, the only finds associated with a stone-built long hall with outbuildings set around a yard were not typically Scandinavian. They include two single-edged knives, a spearhead and four Northumbrian pennies (*stycas*). These suggest a late ninth-century date for occupation, but leave open the possibility that the hall formed part of a native farm built by Anglo-Saxons rather than Vikings.

In Wales the problem of cultural or ethnic identification is particularly acute, because little evidence has been found for buildings or settlements of any type which can be dated to between the ninth and eleventh centuries. An indication of the possible appearance of some structures has been provided by discoveries in Ireland, on the Isle of Man and in the north of England. The remains of numerous timber buildings dating from the tenth to twelfth centuries have been found during excavations in Viking Dublin, densely packed within an urban streetscape. Most had low post-and-wattle walls of hazel, ash or elm, plastered with clay. Although the houses vary in plan (there are five different types), all were rectangular or square, most appear to have had hipped roofs (sloping ends of roofs) rather than gabled-ended (where roof ridge extended to the pointed apex of the end wall), and nearly all were thatched with straw. The bulk of the roof weight was supported by internal posts, and the doors had wooden thresholds with oak jambs on either side. The typical Dublin 'town' house had a wide central aisle, flanked by a raised bench or sleeping area on either side, and the doorway was usually in an end wall. A rectangular stone-kerbed fireplace, where found, was usually located in the centre of the building.

Several forms of town house are known from England. Timber halls, at 'ground level' or 'sunken-floored', often had internal posts which created three aisles, and varied in size from 4-5m in width and between 6-10m in length. The post-and-wattle walled buildings in Anglo-Scandinavian York resemble those in Saxon areas, and many such variations may be determined by the availability of raw materials and regional rather than cultural influences.

107 *Finds within the black earth covering the sunken floor of Building 3, Llanbedrgoch, included this fine bronze buckle of tenth-century type. Length 74.9mm. (NMW 95.46H)*

During this period, a 'sill-beam' construction to carry walls appears to have been used, and examples have been recognised at the urban centres of York, London and Chester, as well as on rural

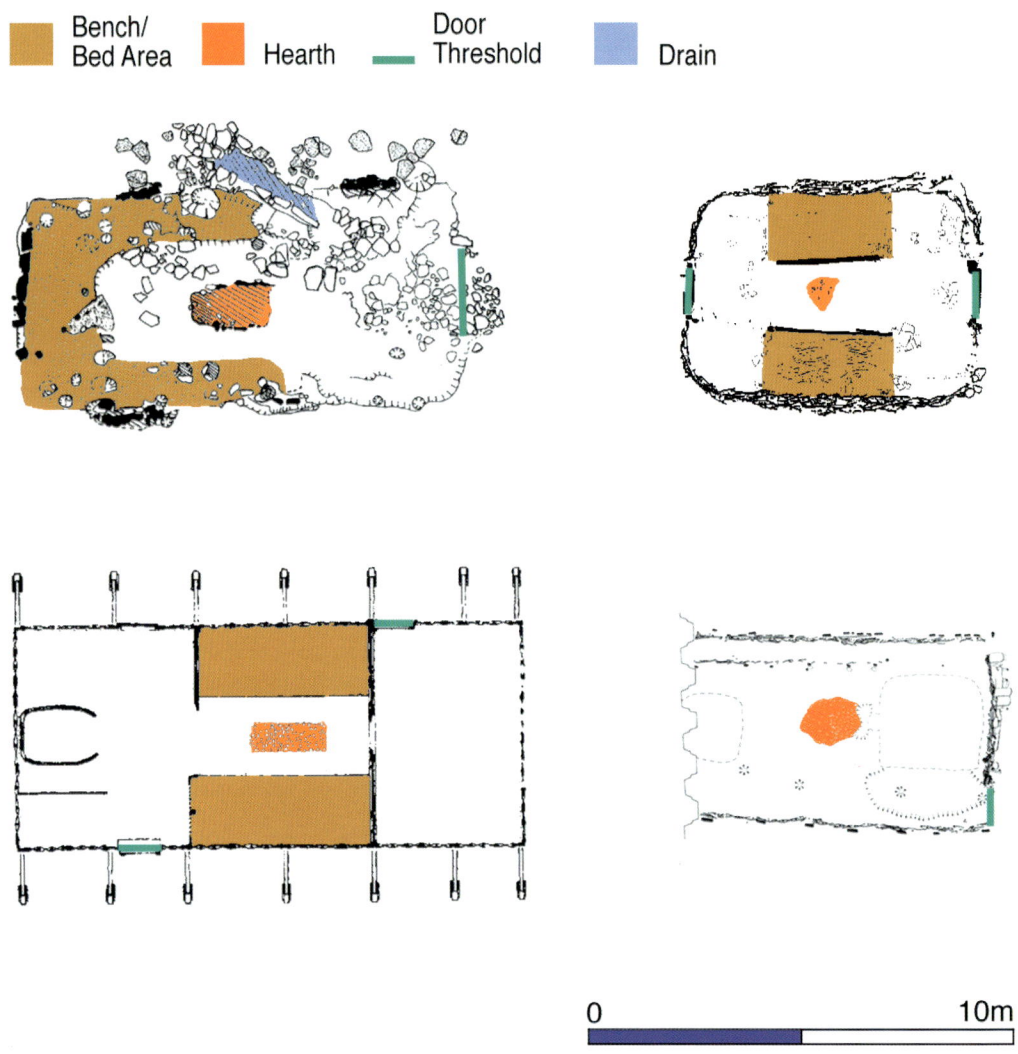

Bench/Bed Area   Hearth   Door Threshold   Drain

0   10m

108   *Viking Age house plans (clockwise from top left): Building 1, Llanbedrgoch, Anglesey; Viking Dublin; Anglo-Scandinavian York; Scandinavian Hedeby, on the southern border of the Danish kingdom.*

sites. At least three of the tenth-century buildings discovered so far at Llanbedrgoch utilised this method of construction. Building 1 was about 11m in length, forming a single room where the whole family slept and ate, worked and entertained. Its principal features were a sunken floor and narrow, low walls of limestone blocks forming a foundation for a timber superstructure. Family and guests sat on simple low benches or wooden platforms (sometimes made of wattle), indicated now by raised areas of natural loam arranged along the walls around three sides of a hearth. This fireplace, central both to the building and to family life, had a carefully laid rectangular setting of kerbstones,

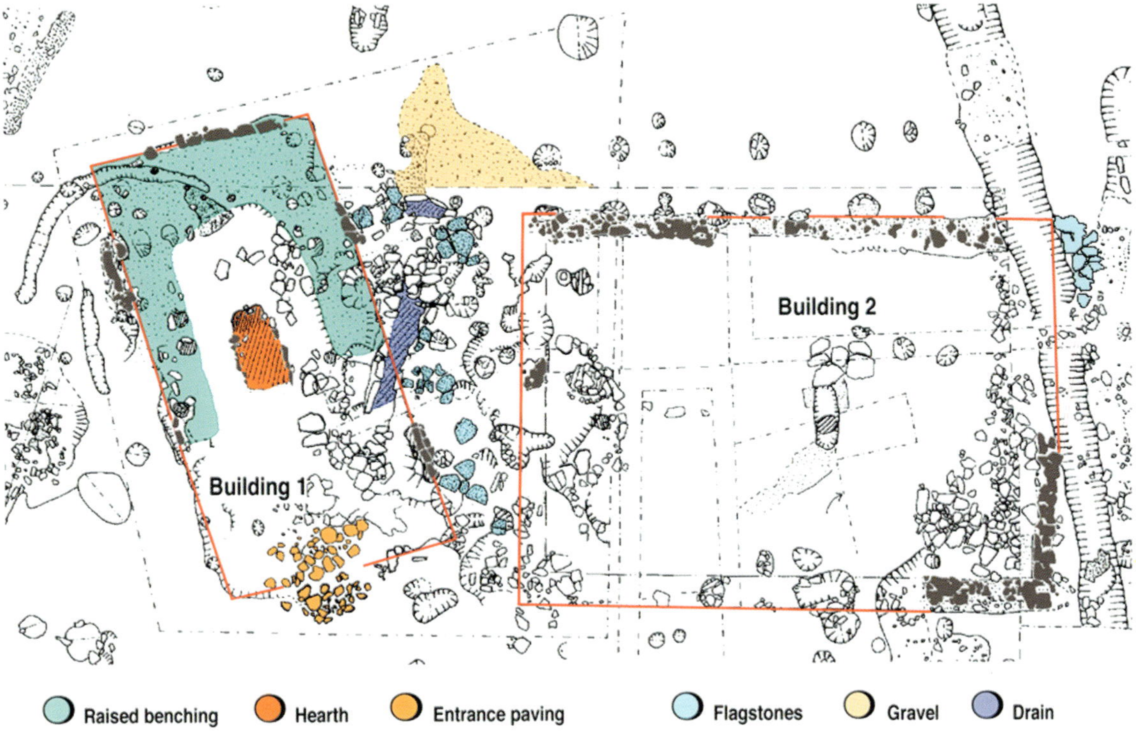

Raised benching — Hearth — Entrance paving — Flagstones — Gravel — Drain

109   Multi-period plan of part of the site at Llanbedrgoch, showing detail of Buildings 1-2.

and showed evidence of long use. Radiocarbon dates obtained from the hearth ash and associated deposits (c. 780-980) have now been refined by archaeomagnetic dating of its fired clay. This established that it was last used between c. 890-970. The floor of the southern half of the building was flagged, and a stone-lined and capped drain kept the interior dry. While the house appears to have had a dwelling space in its northern half, no clear evidence was found for animal stalls or the regular overwintering of cattle or other livestock in the southern half. The floor at the dwelling end was 'clean', in that there was little organic debris or dung of any kind, only ash and charcoal from the fire.

110   Building 1 at Llanbedrgoch. The paved surface can be seen in the foreground.

111 *Sandstone basin or trough, probably for holding water. One half had been incorporated into the floor of Building 1, Llanbedrgoch, probably in the first half of the tenth century. Length about 560mm. (NMW 96.41H/98.50H)*

Cooking

Cooking was done over a central hearth, using a cauldron suspended from a chain to boil broths, or spits and long handled forks for roasting and sometimes in pots. Numerous hooks and line or net sinkers from Viking period settlements illustrate the importance of fishing in fresh and salt water. Meat and fish would have been dried or salted to preserve them over the winter months. Food would have been served in wooden bowls or trenchers, and eaten with the fingers or with the aid of a personal knife. The central role of the hearth in most societies at this time is reflected in the Welsh saga of Heledd, in which her brother Cynddylan, lord of Pengwern (Shrewsbury), is killed by Saxons and his home destroyed. Heledd laments:

'Dark is Cynddylan's hall tonight
With no fire, no songs
My cheek's worn out with tears'
(Anon, ninth century, translation by T. Conran).

112 *The hearth in Building 1, Llanbedrgoch, being sampled for archaeomagnetic dating. This refined the broad radiocarbon dates for the building to c. 890-970.*

113 *Copper alloy suspension hook from a sheet metal cauldron, and rimsherd of a tenth-century jar or cooking pot in Chester ware with sooted surface, suggesting that it may have been placed in the embers of a hearth. Both from Llanbedrgoch, Anglesey. (Left: NMW 95.46H; right: NMW 98.50H)*

114 *Diet varied between regions, depending on the availability of resources. In some areas such as the Faeroe Islands, fishing, wild-fowling and whaling were staple subsistence. In others, the rearing of cattle, sheep, pigs and goats was important (dairy produce, meat and raw materials), while hunting was a common practice. Most of the animal bones at Llanbedrgoch were waste from meals, predominately domestic species such as cattle. Dog bones have also been identified.*

115 *Rotary querns were used for grinding corn to make coarse flour for bread. These examples from Llanbedrgoch are made from local stone (the diameter of complete example 423mm). The combination of both arable and pastoral land use at this site is paralleled in the analysis of pollen grains from samples taken during excavations at Rhuddlan near Denbigh. (NMW 95.46H)*

The adjacent structure, Building 2, was also rectangular, sunken-floored, and 12m long. Its walls used the foundation bed technique recognised elsewhere: a low bedding of stone rubble set within a shallow foundation trench to support a wooden sill-beam. Charcoal samples recovered from the soil over the sunken floor have given a radiocarbon date range of *c*. 855-1000.

Who constructed these buildings? The building layouts show some similarities with contemporary structures in both Scandinavian and Anglo-Saxon regions: for example, low benching has been considered to be a characteristic of Scandinavian buildings. However, essential differences exist in the position of entrances and internal roof supports which may be the components of a building tradition adapted to the local resources and environment. In the absence of more information on Welsh building traditions at this period, it cannot yet be asserted that it represents a native type of building, but it is not unlikely that new features were taken up by the indigenous population as adaptations to local circumstance.

116 *This mollusc feast from the Anglesey shore was found in the fill of an eleventh-century ditch at Llanbedrgoch. Edible cockles and winkles such as these formed an important addition to diet, being a rich local source of protein, mineral salts and vitamins. They were also useful as fishing bait.*

117 *Carbonised grains of barley* (Hordeum sp.) *recovered from the hearth of Building 1, Llanbedrgoch. Together with barley, wheat and oats were an important native crop on Anglesey, dubbed 'Môn mam Cymru', 'Mona the mother of Wales'. The Vikings were also farmers, experienced in cultivating cereal crops such as barley, rye and oats, and vegetables like peas, beans, cabbage and root crops. Fruit such as apples, wild berries and plums was also important.*

118 *A selection of iron knife blades with angle- and straight backs from Llanbedrgoch. The narrow tangs would originally have been fitted with wooden or bone handles. Lengths from 74.5mm – 110.6mm. (NMW 95.46H/96.41H/98.50H)*

Climate
The period from about 700 to 1300 is sometimes called the *'Little Optimum'* Medieval Warm Epoch, when annual summer temperature increased by a few degrees.

Dress

Information about Viking dress comes from contemporary images (often stylised and lacking detail) found on a range of objects, from literary references (most late in date) and from archaeological evidence for clothing and jewellery (sometimes found in graves). The basic garment for men, women and children would have been the tunic, ankle-length for women. Men wore woollen trousers and a shirt, with a brooch or pin to fasten a cloak of wool, sheepskin or fur. Women might wear apron-skirts over their tunics. Cloaks and tunics could be coloured with dyes and edged with decorative tablet woven braids.

The most common dress fastener was the brooch. During the ninth and tenth centuries, shoulder brooches were used by women to fasten the shoulder straps of their tunics. In Scandinavia the

119 Glass beads from Llanbedrgoch, Anglesey. Many different shapes and patterns have been found on Viking period sites. Length of yellow melon bead 24.5mm. (NMW 95.5H/95.46H/98.51H)

120 Viking dress in the tenth century. The woman, shown wearing her best jewellery, finishes some spinning; the merchant weighs out silver on portable scales.

121 Openwork boss from a gilt bronze oval brooch from Llanbedrgoch. The fragment probably formed part of an openwork outer shell which would have covered a plain oval shell and catch-pin. This was one of the most typical types of Scandinavian jewellery for women, and has been regarded as an important indicator of Scandinavian presence (though other explanations for its occurrence may exist). Probably tenth century. (NMW 95.5H)

122 Ringed pin found on the foreshore of the Severn Estuary near Portskewett, Monmouthshire. Late ninth to mid-tenth century. Length 154.5mm. (Newport Museum & Art Gallery; NPTMG 92.16)

domed oval brooch was popular, cast in bronze and ornamented with stylised animals, often embellished with bosses or silver wire. The ringed pins and brooches of Ireland were rapidly adopted by the Vikings for fastening cloaks and were worn either on the right shoulder or centrally. The pins were held in place by a cord tied to the ring and then to the shaft once it had passed through the cloth.

Beads, usually amber or glass, could be strung to hang between pairs of oval brooches or worn as necklaces. Silver arm rings, made from recycled silver and often decorated with a range of punched designs, were portable wealth worn for display and prestige. Combs, toilet equipment, whetstones, small knives and keys were often suspended from a belt.

124 Selection of copper alloy ringed pins from Llanbedrgoch, Anglesey. Tenth century. Length of complete shaft (bent) 143.2mm. (NMW 96.41H)

123 Incomplete copper-alloy penannular brooch of 'ball-type' with plain terminals, from Culver Hole, Llangynydd, on the Gower Peninsula. The distribution of the brooch type centres on areas of Norse settlement in the West and Norway (where many may have been made). Probably first half of the tenth century and of Viking/Irish type. Outer diameter 88mm. (NMW 31.118/2)

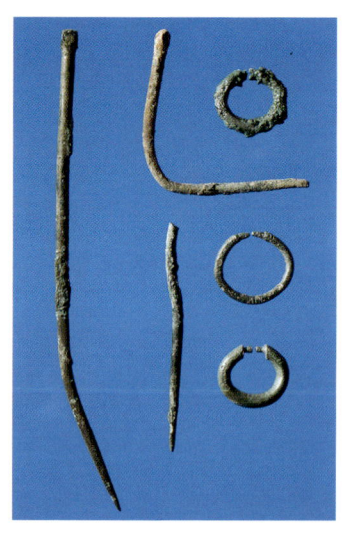

Craft Processes

The Vikings were skilled craftsmen as well as farmers, seafarers and merchants. Towns like Dublin and York attracted craftsmen with varied skills, while market centres were places where manufacture and trade could take place. Llanbedrgoch appears to have been a base for a number of craft activities in the tenth century, for there was a ready market for the products both locally and among the merchants traversing the Irish Sea.

125 Mammal bone and sometimes whale bone or walrus ivory were used in the manufacture of a wide variety of objects. Antler which had been shed and collected could be cut up to make the components of combs and comb cases. The tine tips and brow ridges, such as these offcuts from Building 2, Llanbedrgoch, were usually discarded. (NMW 95.46H)

126 A semi-forged bar end of iron (foreground), together with other fragments of forge waste, reveal the presence of a smithy producing the tools indispensable in daily life. These tools include a fragment of a saw, a hammer-head (length 86mm) and small socketed and tanged chisels. Llanbedrgoch. (NMW 96.41H/98.50H)

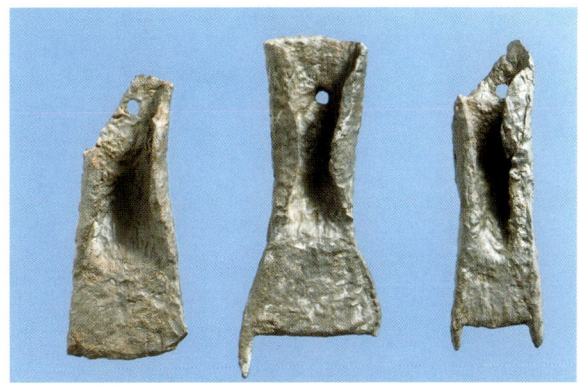

127 Toothed socketed tools associated with leather working have been excavated at Llanbedrgoch. Similar tools are known at a number of early medieval sites in Ireland and England, including Dublin, Whithorn and York. Hides could be turned into a variety of goods such as shoes, sheaths, purses, belts, straps and harnesses. Length of the most complete toothed socketed tool 56.9mm. (NMW 98.50H)

128 Bone and lead spindle whorls from
Llanbedrgoch show that yarn was spun
on site. A few loom weights indicate that
upright looms would have been used to
produce cloth. Woollen cloaks were export
commodities, but most weaving at
Llanbedrgoch may have been for the home
market. The iron pin from Llanbedrgoch
was for stitching, while the glass linen
smoother or 'slick-stone' from Rhuddlan
(on left) would have been used to give a
gloss in the finishing of cloth (usually
linen or fine worsteds) or to smooth
garments after laundering (diameter
77mm). Tenth century. (NMW 95.46H,
98.50H)

129 Silver and bronze casting has been recognised at all
Scandinavian markets. These droplets of silver and copper
alloy and the copper alloy waste sprue, all from
Llanbedrgoch, may derive from the casting of jewellery
and mass-produced ornaments. The small copper alloy
ingot displays small indents from being struck by a small
hammer. (NMW 98.50H/98.51H)

131 Penannular arm-rings, an important product of
Dublin's silversmiths, may also have been made on
Anglesey.

130 Lead trial piece (incomplete) with
stamped decoration and the form of a
broad band arm-ring of Hiberno-
Norse type, from Llanbedrgoch.
Maximum
width
21.8mm.
(NMW
98.51H).

The Sword Smith

Master Bladesmith Frank Craddock was commissioned by the Museum in 1994 to recreate experimentally the process of forging a pattern-welded Viking sword blade and manufacture a decorated guard, based on the find from the Smalls Reef, off the coast of Pembrokeshire. Sagas refer to bright blades with patterns standing forth or proud; such a blade would have been a treasured possession; one was valued, according to a tenth-century Saxon will, at 15 slaves or 120 oxen.

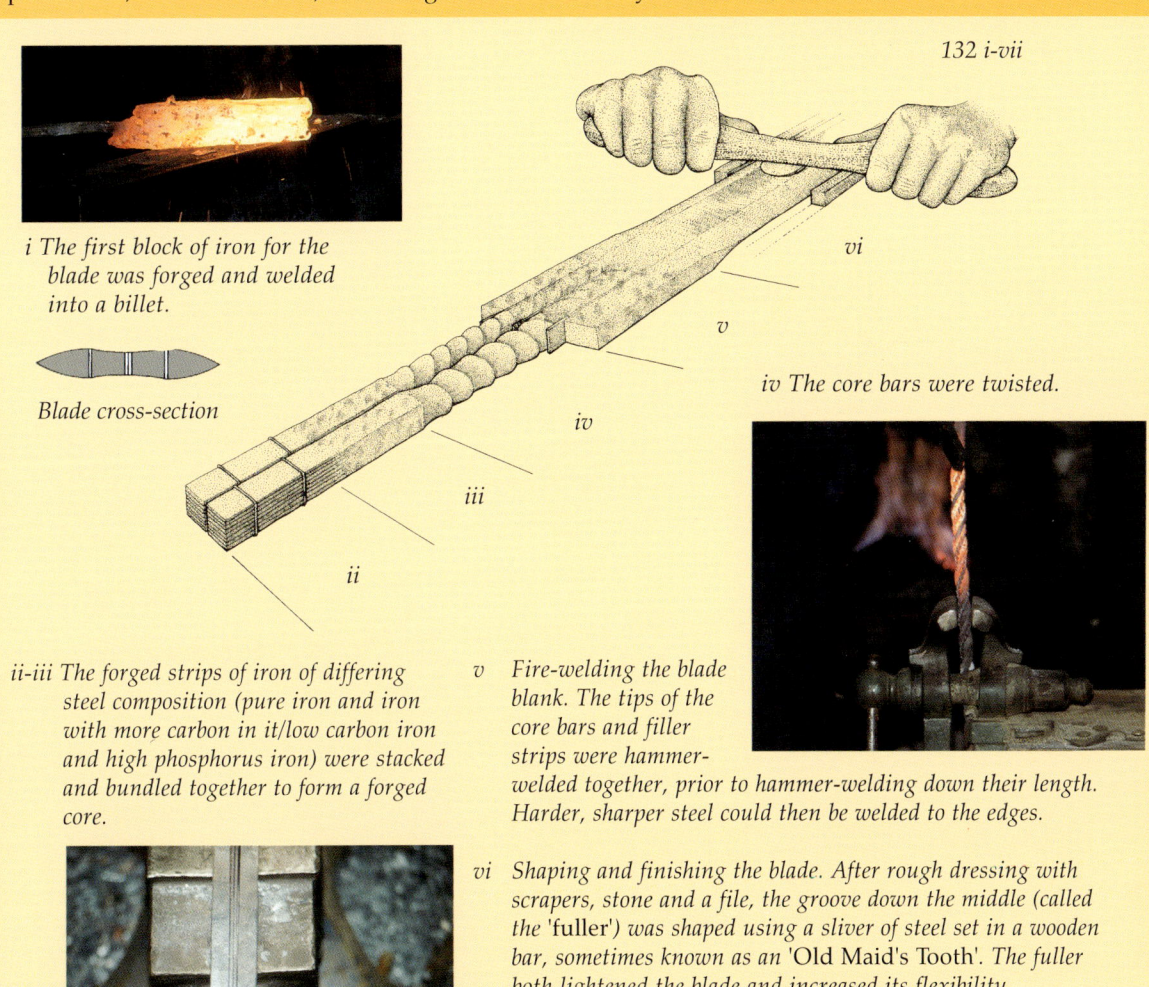

132 i-vii

i The first block of iron for the blade was forged and welded into a billet.

Blade cross-section

iv The core bars were twisted.

ii-iii The forged strips of iron of differing steel composition (pure iron and iron with more carbon in it/low carbon iron and high phosphorus iron) were stacked and bundled together to form a forged core.

v Fire-welding the blade blank. The tips of the core bars and filler strips were hammer-welded together, prior to hammer-welding down their length. Harder, sharper steel could then be welded to the edges.

vi Shaping and finishing the blade. After rough dressing with scrapers, stone and a file, the groove down the middle (called the 'fuller') was shaped using a sliver of steel set in a wooden bar, sometimes known as an 'Old Maid's Tooth'. The fuller both lightened the blade and increased its flexibility.

vii Finally, one of three possible finishing processes was used to bring out the pattern in the blade. A mild organic acid was used to etch the surface, which was occasionally brushed with a feather to ensure an even finish.

ix Once the rough casting had been dressed with files, a design could be marked out and cut with small gravers and chisels. The guard was held firm by a strap attached to the craftsman's foot, against a special sand-filled leather bag.

viii   Casting the guard. A clay core was dipped in wax, which was smoothed to shape. This was enclosed in clay, and the resulting clay mould, once dry, was then heated to melt out the wax and leave a cavity. This was then filled with molten brass.

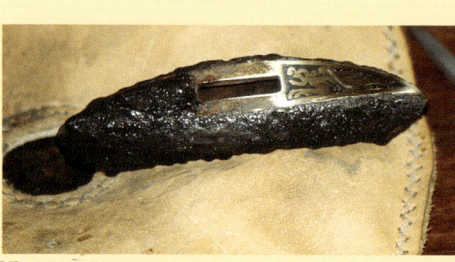

x After the silver wire had been inlaid, the black niello (copper sulphide) could be applied; any surplus was then filed off ready for polishing. (Photographs i-x by F. Craddock)

xi-xii The finished sword replica. The original handle (grip) could have been made of wood, cow horn or leather (some have been found bound with wire). Here, perspex simulates the grip and missing pommel, which would have been decorated in a similar style to the guard.

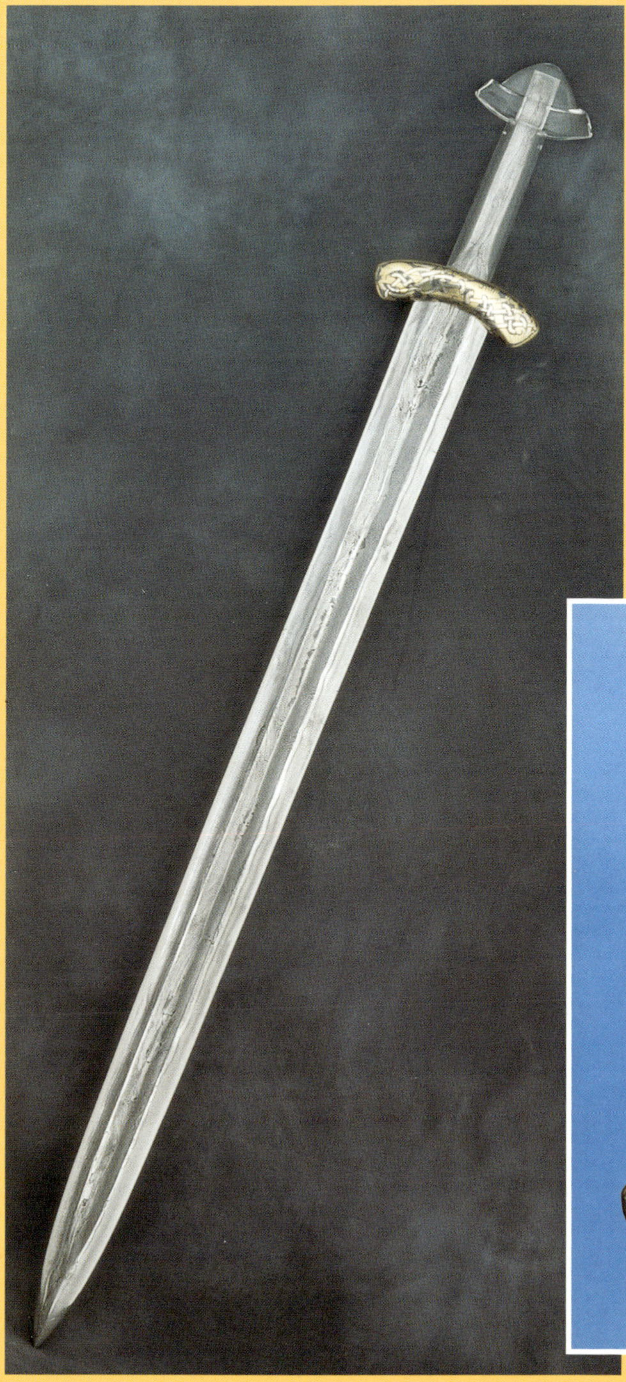

In Old Norse, swords were described in condensed metaphors or 'kennings', such as 'ice of battle', 'fire of the helm','battle needle'. One sword is vividly described in a poem in the poetic Edda, *Helgakviða Hiorvardssonar*: 'a blood-dyed snake lies along the edge, and on the boss a serpent chases its tail'. (Translation by C. Larrington, 1996; by permission of Oxford University Press)

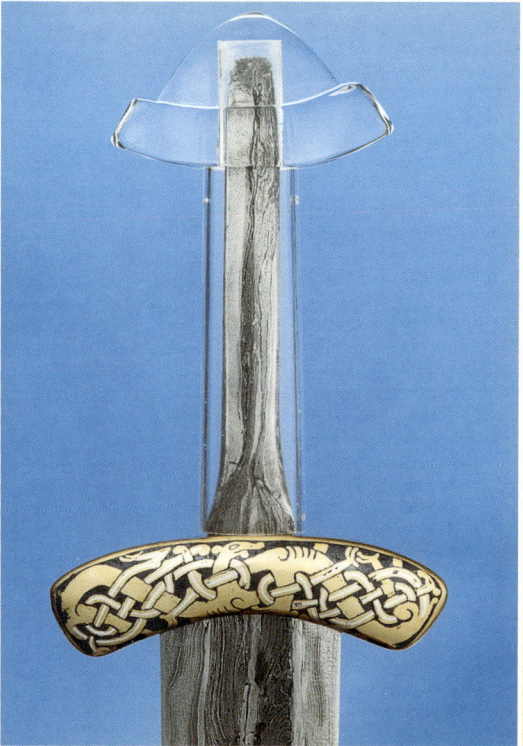

Viking Ornamental Style

Ornament is often the key to recognising the cultural links or origins of the maker or patron. Scandinavian artistic taste and influences in the British Isles can be found on a wide range of objects, many involving animal designs dating to the period following the initial Viking invasions and settlement. The number of such objects from Wales is small, but they reflect a shared fashion or taste around the Irish Sea. A modest influence on sculpture in Wales can also be identified during this period.

The first Viking art style to be introduced into Britain, known as the Borre style (named after the objects found in the ship burial at Borre, Vestfold, Norway), flourished in Scandinavia during the last quarter of the ninth century and much of the tenth century. Two motifs of this style which occur fairly commonly in England and Wales are the so-called 'ring-chain' interlace and, derived from it, a knot pattern. The Borre-style ring-chain motif occurs on stone sculpture on the Isle of Man and in north-west England and north-west Wales. Borre-style ornament is commonly found in England, but present evidence for its adaptation in Ireland is slight, occurring in a derivative form on woodwork and in a few pieces of metalwork.

The presence of this Scandinavian decorative style on some stonework reflects the merging of 'Insular' and Scandinavian influences around the Irish Sea, and the multicultural associations of many craftsmen. It is also evidence of Scandinavian taste (though not extensive) within the Christian community in some parts of Wales. Similar simple 'key' and 'knotwork' patterns are also found on metalwork. Some tenth- or early eleventh-century sculpture in north Wales, such as the crosses at Penmon and Dyserth, is related to sculpture from Cumberland, Westmorland, Lancashire, Cheshire and the Isle of Man.

The next art style, known as Jellinge (named after the site of a royal burial mound in Denmark dendro-chronologically dated to 958/59, which produced a small silver cup decorated with ribbon-like animals), is not common in the Irish Sea area, though it is found on the Isle of Man and in England (generally in a debased version). Some of the best examples of the Mammen art style which followed, named after a decorated axe from Mammen, Jutland, Denmark, can be found on the Isle of Man: the main motif is an asymmetrical animal with body filled with billeting and caught in loop-like scrolls. No objects decorated in Mammen style, which flourished between 950 and 1020, have yet been identified in Wales.

133 Maen Achwyfan *near Whitford, Flintshire. Like a similar cross which once stood at Meliden near Dyserth, it may have acted as a boundary cross. Some of the iconography on the cross is derived from Scandinavian mythology. Tenth or early eleventh century. ECMW 190.*

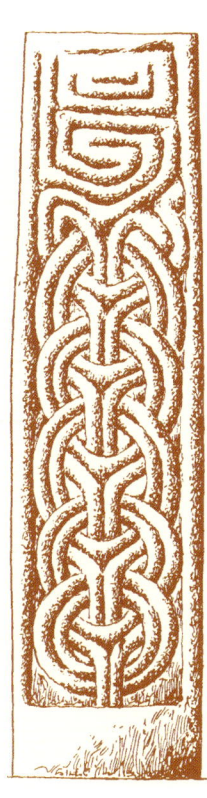

Danish king Cnut, being found on stonework and metalwork from London to Yorkshire. This was followed from the mid-eleventh century to early twelfth century by a more fluid ornament, which takes its name from the woodcarving at the little church at Urnes in Western Norway. Both Ringerike and Urnes styles were adopted in Ireland by indigenous artists experimenting with Irish and Scandinavian designs, and this resulted in a popularisation and adaptation of these styles. The late flourishing of the Urnes style in Ireland saw the creation of exquisite examples of manuscript art and ecclesiastical metalwork, such as the processional cross known as the Cross of Cong, made as a reliquary for a fragment of the True Cross in about 1123.

The evidence for Viking styles in Wales is limited but varied – occurring on some portable objects and a few surviving fixed monuments. The decline of Viking power coincided with the introduction of another artistic style from western Europe which we have come to know since the nineteenth century as the Romanesque.

134 Right: *Borre-style ring-chain or 'vertebral pattern' (looking like a row of interlocking Y-shapes) on a cross shaft at Penmon, Isle of Anglesey (mid-tenth century; ECMW 38). Similar ring-chain motifs can be found on the Isle of Man.* Left: *an interlinked ring-pattern can be seen below the cross-head on one side of the cross known as* Maen Achwyfan. *The continuous ring around the cross and the patterns made up from T-shaped cells also feature on other Viking Age crosses.*

The Ringerike style of animal ornament developed during the first half of the eleventh century from the Mammen-style designs. It was popularly adapted to English tastes during the reign of the

135 *The decoration on this copper alloy buckle from Llanbedrgoch comprises three panels of crosses with pellets in inter-arm spaces, with at one end an animal-headed ('zoomorphic') terminal, and at the buckle end a Borre-style double-strand ring-knot. Tenth century. (NMW 95.46H)*

136 This Scandinavian copper alloy disc brooch in
Jellinge-style, depicting an openwork interlaced
animal, was found during excavations in Chester.
Tenth century. Diameter 31mm. (Drawn by P.
Alebon. Copyright Chester City Council.
Reproduced with permission)

137 The fret patterns which adorn this cross at
Penmon, Anglesey, are Insular in style, but the
'eared' circle-head is Viking in influence, occurring
also in Viking Age Cumbria. Probably tenth
century. ECMW 37.

138 The version of **Urnes** style animal ornament on the Smalls Reef sword guard is reminiscent of the earlier Ringerike style, with tight regular bodies, graceful sinuous loops and symmetry. The workmanship recalls the decoration on the Irish shrine of St Lachtin's arm, and it is likely that it was made in Ireland by highly skilled craftsmen working in 'Hiberno-Viking' style for both secular and ecclesiastical patrons about 1100-25.

139 Pear-shaped stirrup-strap mount with interlaced animal (whose head is at the top of what was once a triangular frame with a circular lug) from Carey, Herefordshire, near the Monmouthshire border. Three rivets once fastened the mount to a leather strap. This Anglo-Scandinavian ornament in Urnes style probably dates to the eleventh century. Surviving height 40mm. (Newport Museum & Art Gallery; NPTMG: 90.5)

140 Copper alloy object in the form of a beast in profile biting its own tail, with niello and silver wire inlay, from Tong, Shropshire. The decoration is 'Sub-Ringerike' in style, and the object may be part of a cheekpiece from an eleventh-century horse harness. Maximum length 33mm. (Private collection; courtesy of Shrewsbury Museums Service)

Pagan Viking Belief

Vikings in the Scandinavian world were pagans, and they had faith in a cycle of cosmological myths about creation and the end of the world and that all things were subject to fate. A Nordic pantheon was well established: most gods and goddesses belonged to the race called *Æsir* who lived in Ásgarth (*Ásgarðr*), while a small group were known as *Vanir*, with differing ways of behaving. The Aesir included *Óthin* (Odin) god of inspiration, power, battle and poetry (his main physical attributes being his cloak, single eye, spear *Gungnir* and horse *Sleipnir*, and ravens on his shoulders); *Thór*, god of strength ('chief giant killer'), thunder and lightning, the elements and crops (his attribute being the axe-hammer *Mjöllni*); and their friend *Loki*, a mischievous figure. The *Vanir* include *Freyr*, god of wealth, fertility, and health (his symbol being a boar), and his sister *Freyja*, a goddess who presided over fertility (with her famous necklace *Brísingamen*). Poems compiled in Iceland (*the Edda*) recount stories of the gods and their myths.

Pendants and figurines have been found in Scandinavia and parts of Britain which are thought to represent some of these gods and their symbols, and narrative scenes found on some carved stone crosses, mainly in England and on the Isle of Man, can be related to episodes in the myths and legends of the Viking homelands.

141 *A detail of the freestanding cross known as* Maen Achwyfan *near Whitford, Flintshire, showing a naked male figure, with a pointed chin and raised arms, holding a spear or staff in his right hand; his other hand holds an axe. On his left hip may be a sword sheath. A meandering ribbon, possibly a snake, encircles his lower body, and spiral-shaped coils surround him. The figural scene would seem to be derived from Scandinavian mythology, though it is not possible to identify it with a specific story (such as the princely warrior Gunnar thrust into a snake pit after his capture by Atli, a scene which was adapted by some artists and sculptors in the north of England and on the Isle of Man).*

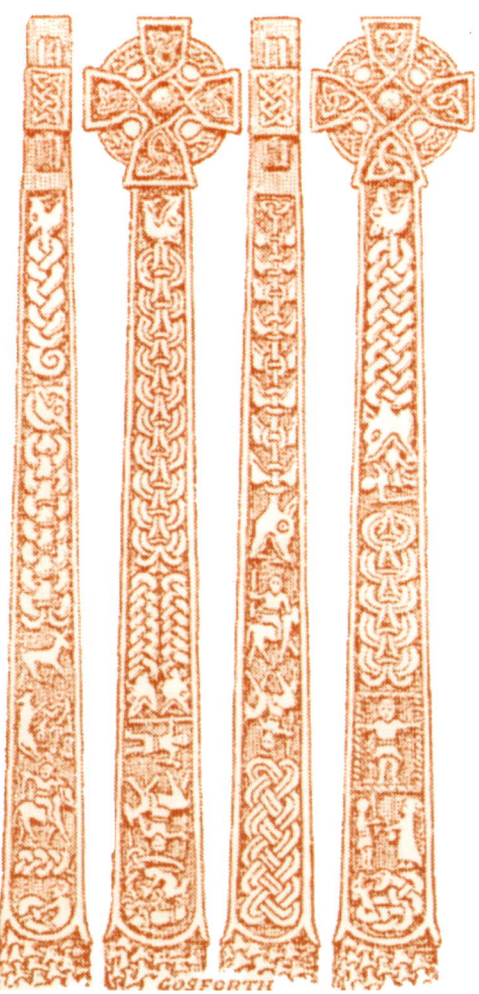

142 *The impressive red sandstone cross in Gosforth churchyard,*
Cumbria, illustrates the assimilation of Scandinavian and
Christian ideas. Christian scenes inspired by
Irish iconography are combined with Scandinavian
ornament and mythical figures: Mary Magdalene appears
as a Valkyrie with pigtailed hair (representing a converted
heathen?) and scenes from Ragnarök *(the tale of the*
overthrow of the Gods of Norse mythology). The decorative
motif on the lower cylindrical part of the shaft is in the
form of Borre-style ring-chain. The cross may have been
commissioned by a local magnate during the first half of
the tenth century. Drawing taken from V.G. Collingwood,
Northumbrian Crosses of the Pre-Norman Age
(London, 1927).

Death and Burial

Pagan Vikings believed in an afterlife, and that the souls of the bravest, heroic fallen warriors would feast in Odin's hall, called in Old Norse *Valhall* ('Hall of the Slain'). This was reflected in their burial customs, for it was common to place in graves everyday objects which might be useful to the dead, such as tools, weapons, and sometimes horses or boats – as much a symbol of status and wealth to the living as of benefit to the dead. Some spectacular burials of chieftains and queens contained boats along with their weapons, jewellery, furnishings, carts and animals. The type of grave, whether pagan or Christian, probably reflects the beliefs of the individual, local burial practice, the beliefs of those undertaking the burial, landmarks or boundary claims.

A scatter of Viking burials occurs on the north and east coasts of Ireland (such as the small cemetery on Rathlin Island), but the only concentrations of settlement and burial yet identified are in Dublin. The cemeteries associated with the Viking 'longphort' established on the River Liffey at Dublin in 841 were found in the modern suburbs of Kilmainham and Islandbridge in the 1840s. The remains of at least thirty-six Viking burials were found in these two cemeteries, dating to the second half of the ninth century. Warriors were buried with swords made on the Continent or in Norway, shields, spears and axes, and brooches made in Scandinavia; women (in the minority) were buried with oval brooches, buckles, needle cases, glass bead necklaces and there is also a whalebone ironing board. Iron tongs or pincers and hammers are thought to indicate the graves of a number of craftsmen, while shears may have accompanied women. Some weapons had been bent or broken – possibly ritually 'killed' to render them useless

(an action often associated with cremations). There is some evidence for an unknown number of native Irish burials in the same area.

Some impressive burials are thought to be those of original land-takers who held estates. Rich pagan Viking graves probably dating to the late ninth or early tenth centuries have been found on the Isle of Man, including a boat burial at Balladoole which contained the remains of a warrior and woman (see p. 57). A middle-aged woman of high social standing, buried in the tenth century with numerous grave goods and wearing an exotic bead necklace, was found during excavations on St Patrick's Isle, Peel, Isle of Man, in the 1980s. In England, graves of similar character have been found in Cumbria. One such Viking warrior's grave at Aspatria, near Carlisle, discovered in 1789, contained a spear with silver adorned socket, a sword with decorated hilt, an axe, parts of a shield, an iron bridle bit and prick spur, a gold buckle and Carolingian-style strap-end. Another Cumbrian warrior grave with grave goods at Hesket-in-the-Forest, may have been a cremation burial.

In Wales, evidence for at least four possible pagan Scandinavian burials of the Viking period have been discovered, though they were not scientifically excavated. All the graves, which may originally have been marked or visible in some way, were located close to the coast.

In the 1930s a Viking grave was found during the excavation of a cess pit for a new house near Talacre, Flintshire. The slab-lined grave, previously concealed beneath windblown sand, lay on top of harder shingle. The sides were made of irregularly-shaped stone slabs, the ends were each formed by single slabs, and the lid was composed of three large slabs. The skeleton was complete, and lay on

Viking Burials • **Hogback Stone**

143 *The location of possible Viking burials in Wales. Contrary to opinion in the 1890s, there is no evidence that the human thigh bones discovered walled up in pillar cavities in the church at Steynton, Pembrokeshire, were those of Viking warriors.*

The Benllech Burial

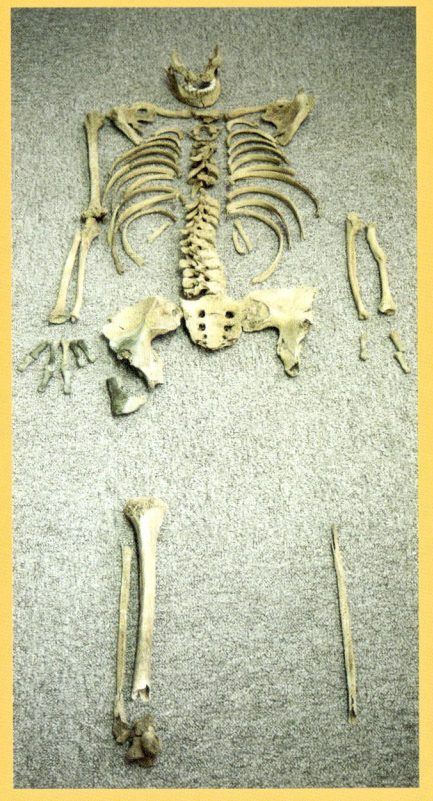

144   *In 1945 a grave was found near this spot on a sandy ridge*
facing Benllech Sands, on the east side of Anglesey. A number of
iron nails and a fragment of antler comb found in it pointed to
the Viking period. Was this person one of the first generation
pagan Viking settlers on Anglesey? Only further research will
tell.

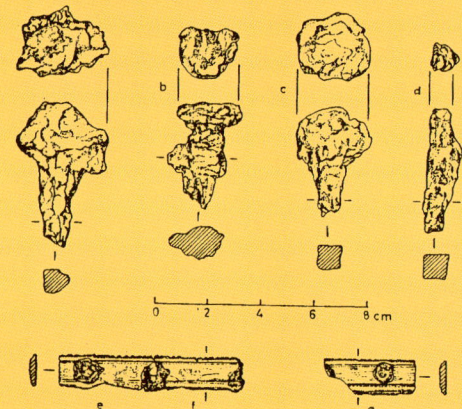

147   *It has been suggested that this is the skeleton*
found in the 1940s in a grave at Benllech,
Anglesey. (Oriel Ynys Môn L2/95)

145   *Fragments of comb and iron nails from the grave*
at Benllech, Anglesey. A slight discolouration on
one of the finger bones was taken as evidence for
the former presence of a ring. (Bangor Museum
& Art Gallery 1984/17.1-7)

146   *The staining of the pelvis and hand of the*
skeleton thought to come from the grave at
Benllech, Anglesey. (Oriel Ynys Môn L2/95)

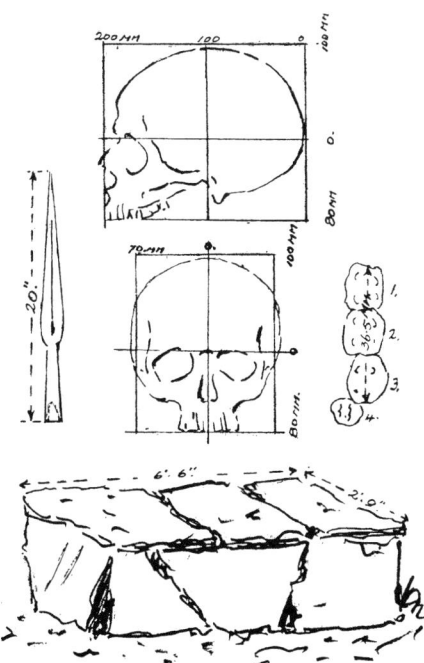

148 *Sketches of the stone cist, skull, dentition and spear from the Viking inhumation at Talacre, Flintshire (reproduced from* Proceedings of the Llandudno, Colwyn Bay and District Field Club *17, 1931-2). The grave, coupled with the sculptural and place-name evidence, suggests Scandinavian activity in the vicinity connected with that in west Cheshire and the Wirral.*

its back, with an iron spearhead 'among the long bones'. An iron knife was also reported from the grave. The present whereabouts of these grave-goods remains unknown.

Another burial at Benllech on Anglesey was investigated in the 1940s. The head of the skeleton lay to the north or north-east, and iron nails suggested the presence of a coffin or chest. The only object to survive in the grave was a fragmentary double-sided antler comb of a type found in the graves of both sexes. The original study of the skeleton reported that the bones were

those of a young woman, and that a slight discolouration on one of the finger bones suggested the former presence of a ring, which no longer survives. Subsequently the artefacts came into the possession of Bangor Museum, but the bones were already lost. A skeleton has recently come to light which may prove to be the missing body. Anatomical examination has established that it is female and aged between 25-35 years. However, the green staining on some of the bones appears to be more extensive than that indicated in the original report, covering an area of the right pelvis and all of the finger bones of the right hand. There is also a healed fracture of the left radius (lower arm) not commented on in the original publication. If the skeleton is of late ninth- or tenth-century date, then the staining may be the result of corrosion of a copper alloy object placed in the grave, such as a ring, buckle or dislodged item of jewellery (as in the case of a burial at Reay in Caithness, where a ringed pin was found above the right thigh).

A third possible late ninth- or early tenth-century pagan grave has been proposed as a likely context for a pair of stirrups found in the nineteenth century at St Mary Hill in the Vale of Glamorgan. A spear and axe found at Caerwent, Monmouthshire, possibly of late ninth/tenth-century date, may have come from a fourth grave. Weapons thought to come from Viking graves have been found in English and Manx churchyards, and the Caerwent findspot lies on the northern edge of the early medieval intra-mural cemetery associated with the *clas* or monastery of the Irish Saint Tatheus. Excavations at Tŷ Newydd on Bardsey Island (*Ynys Enlli*) have also uncovered a cemetery. One of the graves was that of an adult male buried with a silver penny of Edgar (pre-973) in his mouth, apparently respecting the pagan custom of paying the ferryman of the dead his fare for carrying him across the river of Death. A similar practice has been noted in a mid-tenth century grave of a child

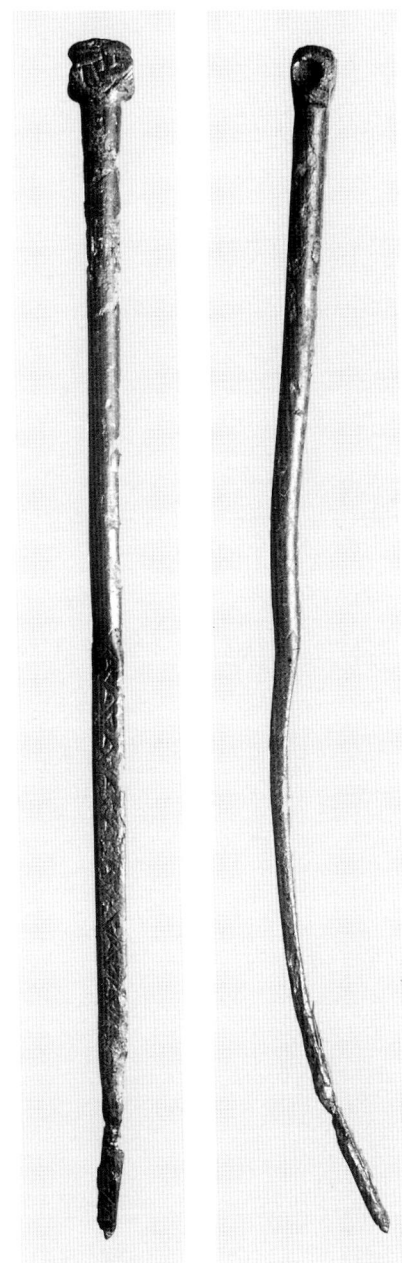

on St Patrick's Isle, Peel, Isle of Man, where a coin was found under the right side of the jaw. The precise historical context of the Bardsey example, thought not to have been buried before about 980, is still under investigation.

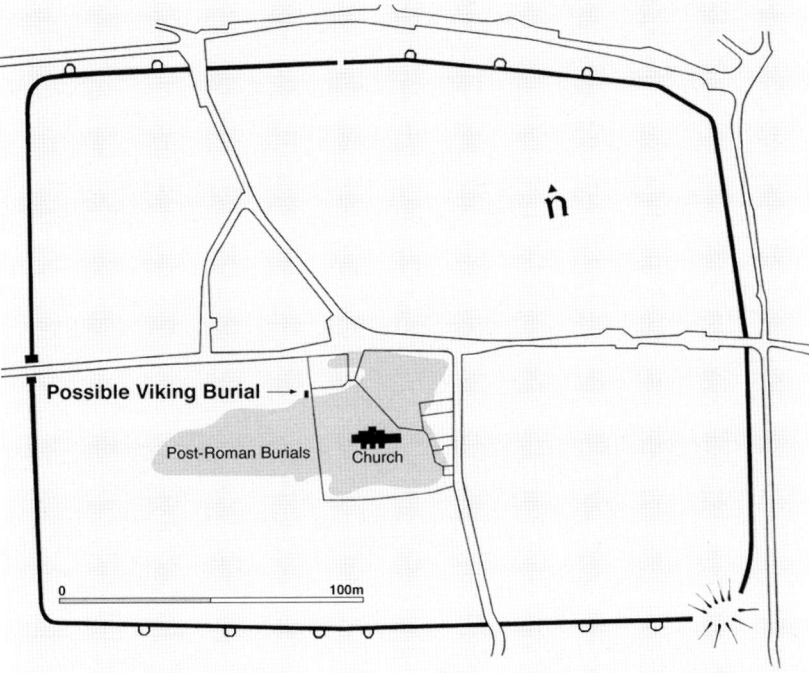

150 *Location of the possible Viking burial at Caerwent, Monmouthshire. The excavation of Insula XII in the area of the Viking grave was halted in 1912 because of the enormous number of other (non-Viking) burials encountered.*

149 *Copper alloy pin with a step pattern on the shaft from Llanfairpwllgwyngyll, Anglesey. Part of a tenth-century ringed pin, it was found during grave-digging in the churchyard in the 1940s, and may have came from a Viking period grave, though not necessarily that of a Viking. Length 152mm. (Oriel Ynys Môn 65/92)*

Vikings as Christians

At the beginning of the ninth century, the Vikings were one of the last pagan peoples of Europe. Their travels, as seafarers, raiders, merchants or settlers, brought them more frequently into contact with Christians, and Viking traders often accepted the Christian faith in order to foster their relationships with clients. The limited number of pagan Viking burials with grave goods in Britain is thought to reflect the rapid adoption by Vikings of Christianity, or at least of local burial customs.

Pagan rites and the practice of burying objects in graves gradually ceased in the course of the tenth century, and this might hint at a more complex relationship between Vikings and the local populations than is generally believed. The influence of local Christians on Viking settlers and intermarriage resulted in a fusion of beliefs. This is reflected by the scenes from pagan Norse myths

151   The hogback at the pre-Norman church at Llanddewi Aber-arth, Ceredigion, is the only example (incomplete) of this Anglo-Scandinavian form of monument to be identified in Wales. The stone, which may once have functioned as a grave-marker, takes the form of a house with a plain gable end. The upper faces are decorated with ribbing representing the roofing depicted on earlier hogbacks (in this case unpatterned by shingle). Probably tenth or eleventh century. Length about 620mm. ECMW 114.

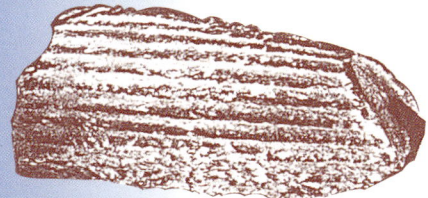

which appear on Christian sculptured stones. On the Isle of Man, tenth-century runic inscriptions appear on Christian cross slabs, and the erection of memorial stones with Celtic and Norse names points to intermarriage with local Christians. Some stone sculpture and metalwork from Wales may reflect similar cultural interchange between Norse and native Welsh. Chester was a busy centre of carving, and the sculptors were influenced by late ninth- and tenth-century Borre and Jellinge styles of Viking art.

152   The Danish settlers of East Anglia issued coins commemorating martyred Christian King Edmund, only some 20 years after they had killed him. The 'St Edmund' penny points to a wide acceptance of the new faith. (NMW 79.94H/4)

The distinctive 'hogback' tombstone, which some have described as a type of Viking colonial monument, originated during the tenth century in areas of Scandinavian settlement in northern England. From there it spread to Scotland and Wales, with only one example surviving from Ireland. There are important collections of such sculpture at Brompton near Northallerton (Yorkshire), Gosforth and Penrith (Cumbria) and Govan (Glasgow), amongst other places. The form of the hogback tombstone was probably inspired by house- or casket-shaped grave covers or reliquaries, and is closely modelled on contemporary houses with gables and often a checked (wooden shingle) roof. Hogbacks are rarely found in situ, most having been re-used in the construction of Norman churches. Little remains of the original vivid polychrome colour schemes, and on many the detail is difficult to interpret.

Runes

Runes are the characters of a script, rather than a language. They are angular letters composed of straight lines, ideal for incising on wood, bone, metal or stone.

153 *This shows one version of the Scandinavian runic alphabet or* futhark, *named after its initial six letters. Anglo-Saxons first brought the script to England; the later Scandinavian* futhark *spread over Europe between the ninth and eleventh centuries.*

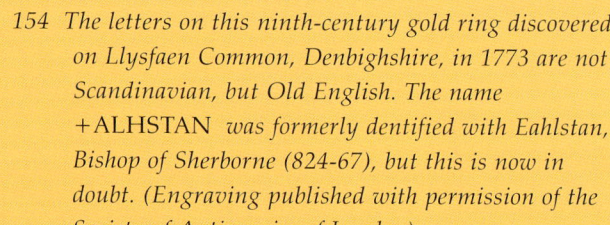

154 *The letters on this ninth-century gold ring discovered on Llysfaen Common, Denbighshire, in 1773 are not Scandinavian, but Old English. The name* +ALHSTAN *was formerly dentified with Eahlstan, Bishop of Sherborne (824-67), but this is now in doubt. (Engraving published with permission of the Society of Antiquaries of London)*

A Runic Riddle

For nearly 50 years the faint marks on the northern face of the eleventh- or twelfth-century cross shaft in the churchyard at Corwen, Denbighshire, have teased many observers. The marks were first mentioned by Professor R.A.S. Macalister in 1935, who suggested that they were capable of interpretation as runes reading I Th FUS, an Old Norse personal name. V.E. Nash-Williams, author of *The Early Christian Monuments of Wales* (1950), believed that the widely spaced marks were traces of a key-pattern or similar design.

If the marks, which span the shaft but are now difficult to see, are runes (this is unclear), they could be Anglo-Saxon, for runes were also used in England. There is nothing to support the suggestion that the supposed 'runes' were carved by a wandering Viking.

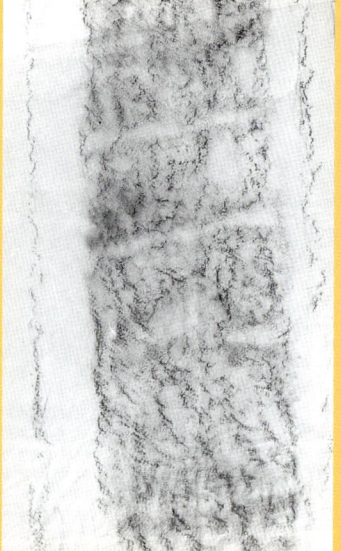

155   *The cross at Corwen, with a rubbing of the marks on its northern face*

The End in Wales

With the death of Cnut in 1035, his Anglo-Scandinavian Empire began to fragment, and Welsh affairs merged with the prelude to the Norman Conquest of England, which began in 1066. In the years following the battle of Hastings, English rebellions were supported by Vikings (such as Harold's sons raiding Bristol and Somerset in 1067). As recorded in the unique *Life of Gruffudd ap Cynan (Historia Gruffud vab Kenan)*, Wales (in particular the north) was closely involved politically and commercially with the Hiberno-Norse world. In 1138 Gruffudd ap Cynan's sons Owain Gwynedd and Cadwaladr brought a fleet of fifteen Norse ships (probably from Ireland) to campaign against the Normans in Ceredigion, which resulted in the sack of St Dogmaels Abbey. Such Viking raids petered out during the first half of the twelfth century, some of the last raids being those of the Orkney Viking Svein Ásleifarson (died 1171).

Scandinavian cultural influence continued to a limited extent in some areas following the Norman advance, which by the 1080s extended well into

156 *Romanesque doorways were often capped by semi-circular slabs* (tympana) *which were ideal for sculptural decoration. This mid-twelfth century tympanum at Penmon, Anglesey, depicts a beast in profile with head turned backwards, biting its own tail which passes between its hind legs. Three-strand interlace forms a border motif. The design is strongly influenced by Insular sculpture, and shows how craftsmen continued to work with old traditions well into the twelfth century.*

Wales. In Ireland, the Viking Age proper is considered to end about 1080, but Norse culture flourished in certain coastal areas well into the twelfth century and Dublin was still Norse speaking at the time of the

Anglo-Norman invasion launched from Wales in 1169-70. In some parts of Wales, Viking influence may also have lingered. On the Continent, the long-term consequence of Viking settlement in France had been the establishment of the Duchy of Normandy by the 'Northmen' in the tenth century. In an indirect way, one of the greatest Viking legacies for England and Wales was the Norman invasion, marking the dawn of a new era.

157 *The Normans took over a land of complex artistic traditions. A remarkable example is the decoration influenced by the late Viking* Urnes *style which can be found just across the border in the Old Red Sandstone decoration of the church of St Mary and St David, Kilpeck, Herefordshire. The ornament on the church, which was probably constructed under Hugh, Lord of Kilpeck, in the 1130s, represents a local fusion of Scandinavian, Romanesque and Anglo-Saxon styles.*

158 *Illustration from G.R. Lewis,* Illustrations of Kilpeck Church, Herefordshire: in a series of drawings made on the spot *(London, 1842), showing the decoration of the south door.*

The Legacy

The Viking impact on Wales has to be seen as part of a broader pattern of activity in north-west Europe and is comparable, for instance, with that on Brittany. There was little impact on the Welsh language and political structures, and the Vikings initiated no urban developments. The Welsh were effective in limiting Viking settlement, and the Vikings can be credited with indirect influence on the development of a sense among the Welsh of solidarity against an external threat. Some of their episodic impact is now invisible – the loss of treasures and the cultural damage caused by this plundering – although largely documented through the annals, place-names and occasional finds. Following recent excavations this can now be viewed in a new light.

Vikings reached North America to the West and worked for the Emperor in Constantinople (*Byzantium*, now Istanbul) to the East; they continue to exert a fascination for people around the world, encouraged by a persistent romantic image of the proud Northern race, but tempered in recent decades by new perspectives of both a darker side and more cultured aspects. The physical evidence of a Scandinavian presence in Wales remains sparse, but public interest in the Vikings is considerable: two re-enactment groups

have adherents committed to replicating costume accurately through revived crafts and entertaining the public with 'living history' and the period features in the National Curriculum for Wales. For many, the quest for Vikings in Wales continues.

159   Re-enactment group at the Museum of Welsh Life, St Fagans (above) and in Cathays Park, Cardiff (below).

160   Detail of a bronze handrail in the form of a Viking ship on the grand staircase, Swansea Guildhall (built 1932-36). Scandinavian links with Swansea embellish the grand staircase, with masks of Svein Forkbeard and his warriors adorning the keystones, while the bronze handrails of the staircase are in the form of the bows and sterns of his longships.

Museums and Monuments to Visit

This is just a selection of the many museums, libraries and sites holding manuscripts or objects which relate to the Viking period in Wales:

Aberystwyth: National Library of Wales, Aberystwyth, Ceredigion, SY23 3BU

Bangor: Bangor Museum & Art Gallery, Ffordd Gwynedd, Bangor, LL57 1DT

Cardiff: National Museum & Gallery, Cathays Park, Cardiff, CF10 3NP

Llangefni: Oriel Ynys Môn (Anglesey Heritage Gallery), Llangefni, Isle of Anglesey, LL57 7TQ

Newport: Newport Museum & Art Gallery, John Frost Square, Newport, NP9 1PA

Welshpool: Powysland Museum & Montgomeryshire Canal Centre, The Canal Wharf, Welshpool, SY21 7AQ

Crosses:

Carew, Pembrokeshire

Dyserth, near Prestatyn, Denbighshire

Maen Achwyfan, near Whitford, Flintshire

Nevern, Pembrokeshire

Penmon Priory, Isle of Anglesey

St David's, Pembrokeshire

Other collections:

Chester: Grosvenor Museum

Dublin: National Museum of Ireland

Edinburgh: National Museum of Scotland

Isle of Man: Manx National Heritage, Manx Museums, Douglas

London: The British Museum, The Victoria and Albert Museum, The Museum of London, The British Library

Oxford: Ashmolean Museum

York: Yorkshire Museum; Jorvik Centre

Summary List of Silver Hoards Found in Wales

1   Minchin Hole, Gower, Swansea. Deposited *c*. 850 (Swansea Museum).

2   Llanbedrgoch, Isle of Anglesey. Deposited *c*. 850 (National Museum & Gallery Cardiff).

3   Red Wharf Bay silver armlets, Isle of Anglesey. Deposited by *c*. 905 (National Museum & Gallery Cardiff).

4   Bangor 'Midland Bank', High St, Gwynedd. Deposited *c*. 925 or shortly after (Bangor Museum & Art Gallery, Bangor; loaned to National Museum & Gallery Cardiff).

5   Bangor 'Senior Vicar's Garden', Gwynedd. Deposited *c*. 970 (missing).

6   Laugharne, Carmarthenshire. Deposited *c*. 975 (private collection).

7   Near Monmouth, Monmouthshire. Deposited 990s (missing).

8   Penrice, Gower, Swansea. Deposited *c*. 1008 (location unknown).

9   Drwsdangoed, Gwynedd. Deposited *c*. 1030 (location unknown).

10   Bryn Maelgwyn, Conwy. Deposited *c*. 1024 (National Museum & Gallery Cardiff).

11   Pant-yr-eglwys, nr. Llandudno, Conwy. Deposited 1020s (National Museum & Gallery Cardiff).

Glossary and Abbreviations

Æsir	Race of Norse gods, including Odin and Thor.
Anglo-Saxon Chronicle	Annual record of events, in English, and begun during the reign of Alfred the Great (871-99).
Anglo-Scandinavian	Used to describe the cultural mix which followed the ninth-century settlement in north and east England.
Annals	Yearly entries in an annual record of events.
Annular	In the form of a ring.
Anthropomorphic	Of human form and character.
Billet	Small bar of metal.
Black Gentiles	Also known as Dubgaill, 'black foreigners', for the Danes (many based in York).
Borre	Viking art style named after burial mound in Denmark. Geometric interlace motifs favoured. Flourished in the late ninth-tenth century.
Brycheiniog	Small early medieval kingdom in south-central Wales, roughly equivalent to the later shire county of Breconshire.
Burh	Anglo-Saxon fortified centre or township. Many were set up to counter the Danish threat.
Carolingian	Name of the ruling dynasty that replaced the Merovingians on the Continent. Used generally to mean the period *c.* 750-900 in Western Europe.
Chronicle	A continuous record of events in order of time.
Clenched nails	Used to join overlapping (clinker) planks. Comprises an iron nail with large head, driven through a rectangular or diamond-shaped rove or washer, and deformed so that it cannot be withdrawn.
Clinker	Method of constructing boats with overlapping planks.
Crop marks	Light and dark marks seen in growing and ripening crops, reflecting differences in the soil, buried walls or pits and ditches.
Danegeld	Annual taxation (*heregeld*) instituted in 1012 to pay Scandinavian mercenaries.
Danelaw	Area of north and east England under Scandinavian control and following Scandinavian law.
Deheubarth	Literally 'southern parts'. For most periods, equivalent to Dyfed, Ceredigion, Ystrad Dywi and Brycheiniog.
Dendrochronology	Tree-ring dating of wood. Calculation of the felling date of a tree by measuring the size of the annual growth rings, which vary according to conditions.
Ealdorman	An Anglo-Saxon noble or man of high rank; an administrative official.
Earl	English title of nobility, from Old Norse *jarl*.
ECMW	Abbreviation for V. E. Nash-Williams 1950, *The Early Christian Monuments of Wales*, Cardiff. The number which follows is the catalogue entry of the stone.

Fuller	Longitudinal groove down the length of a sword blade to make it lighter and more flexible.
Futhark	The runic alphabet, named after the first six symbols.
Gafol	Old English word for tribute paid to Viking armies.
Geophysical surveying	Surveying the physics of the earth, often with magnetometer or resistivity.
Hack-silver	Fragments of silver used as bullion. Usually cut up from brooches, arm-rings, ingots and coins.
Heregeld	'Army tax'. Annual taxation instituted in 1012 to pay Scandinavian mercenaries.
Hogback	Recumbent stone monument with arched back, resembling a hog or hall roof.
Insular	Belonging to the style of early medieval culture of Ireland and Britain.
Hiberno-Norse	Term used to describe cultural mix following the ninth-century Hiberno-Viking Scandinavian settlement in Ireland (*Hibernia* = Ireland).
Jellinge	Viking art style named after designs found on a silver cup in a royal burial chamber at Jellinge, Denmark. Flourished in the tenth century.
Llys/Llysoedd (pl.)	Welsh term for Court.
Longphort	Naval encampment.
Loom-weight	Weight made of fired clay or stone, to tension the vertical threads on a loom.
Maenol/Maenolydd (pl.)	Welsh term corresponding roughly to an English 'manor'.
Maerdref/Maerdrefi (pl.)	Welsh term for the townland surrounding the court, held in demesne by the lord.
Magnetometer	Measures very small variations in the earth's magnetic field caused by buried features.
Mammen	Viking art style, named after ornament on the Mammen axe. Developed during the second half tenth/early eleventh century.
Midden	A heap or deposit of rubbish.
Niello	A black inlay made from a compound of copper or silver sulphide, usually applied to metalwork.
Quernstone	Disc-shaped stone for grinding grain by hand.
Penannular	Incomplete ring. Used to describe a type of brooch which has a gap in the hoop between two terminals.
Posthole	Hole cut in ground for vertical wooden post (usually missing or decayed) which once supported a structure. Usually recognised by the distinctive character of the soil filling the hole.
Pseudo-penannular	Used to describe a form of brooch which resembles the penannular form, but in which the gap in the hoop is closed by a small decorative 'bridge'.
Radiocarbon dating	Dating technique which measures the amount of radiocarbon (C14) in organic matter such as wood and bone.
Ragnarök	The end of the world of the pagan Scandinavian gods.
Reeve	Old English word for official of high rank, having local jurisdiction under the king.

Revetment	A retaining wall or fence to prevent slipping of a steep or vertical face.
Ringerike	Viking art style which flourished in the first half of the eleventh century, named after an area in Norway rich in stone carvings in this style.
Romanesque	Style of architecture and art dominant in Western Europe during the twelfth century.
Runes	Script of characters made of straight lines.
Saga (Old Norse)	Originally meant 'what is said', but the word came to mean a prose narrative written in the twelfth century or later.
Sceat/Sceatta	Small silver coin minted in southern England and Frisia in the eighth century.
Spindlewhorl	Small perforated weight of bone, pottery, stone or lead. Fitted onto a spindle, it acted as a flywheel to assist the spinning of wool thread.
Sprue	Piece of metal attached to a casting, after solidifying in a mould channel.
Stratigraphy	Principle adopted from geology. The way in which one or more deposits overlie another to form a sequence.
Styca	Small copper coin (penny) made in ninth-century Northumbria.
Trial Piece	Also called 'motif piece', on which craftsmen practised a design; sometimes made of lead, on which a die or punch has been tested.
Urnes	The final Viking art style, named after a decorated wooden church at Urnes, Norway. Developed in the second half of the eleventh century and continued into the twelfth century.
Viking Age	Period of Scandinavian history from the late eighth to the eleventh centuries. Begins with the first Viking raids on western Europe.
Zoomorphic	In the likeness of an animal (or part of one).

Acknowledgements

Tony Daly of the Department of Archaeology & Numismatics, NMGW, was responsible for producing most of the artwork and preliminary layout (figures 2, 17, 26, 27, 28, 31, 37, 42, 43, 50, 53, 54, 60, 64, 71, 73, 74, 75, 76, 86, 87, 98, 105, 108, 109, 120, 132, 138, 143, 150, 153).

The Photography Department, NMGW (in particular Kevin Thomas and Jim Wild) were responsible for figures 9, 15, 16, 22, 24, 29, 30, 32-34, 41, 45-47, 49, 51, 52, 55-57, 59, 61-63, 66-68, 70, 72, 81-85, 90c-d, 94, 99, 107, 110, 111, 113-119, 121-131, 132 xi-xii, 135, 139, 149, 151, 152, 157, 158, 160. Figures 18, 20 were taken by the Department of Geology. Figures 3, 13, 21, 25, 35, 36, 38, 39, 48, 69, 77, 79, 88, 89, 91-93, 94-96, 100, 101-104, 106, 112, 133, 134, 137, 141, 144, 146, 147, 155, 156, 159 are by the author. Many of the illustrated objects have undergone conservation in the skilled hands of Mary Davis, Penny Hill and Louise Mumford.

Every attempt has been made to contact copyright owners. Where unsuccessful, the National Museums & Galleries of Wales would appreciate any information that would enable it to do so.

I am grateful to the following individuals and institutions for allowing the permission to photograph objects in their ownership or care: Bangor Museum & Art Gallery (62, 83); Newport Museum & Art Gallery (32, 66, 122, 139); Oriel Ynys Môn (Anglesey Heritage Gallery), Llangefni, Isle of Anglesey (146, 147); I. Carruthers; Dr J. Davis (29); Powysland Museum & Montgomeryshire Canal Centre, Welshpool (34).

I would also like to thank the following institutions for permission to reproduce illustrative material: the Cambrian Archaeological Association (7, 11), Chester City Council (40, 136), The British Library (44, 58); The Gwynedd Archaeological Trust (64); RCAHMW (19, 65, 97); The National Library of Wales (1, 6); Newport Museum & Art Gallery (80); Shrewsbury Museums Service (140); The Society of Antiquaries, London (154), Dr David Griffiths (87).
My special thanks to Mr J. Bond and Mr David Greenhalgh, *Grunal Moneta*, for appearing in 69 and 84, 131 respectively.

During the preparation of this book I have had cause to consult many colleagues who have advised on particular matters, and to whom I owe thanks: Dr Lesly Abrams; Eva Bredsdorff; Alison Brigstocke; Irene Carruthers; Frank Craddock; David Freke; Dr Gillian Fellows-Jensen; Dr David Griffiths; Alun Gruffudd; Dr Richard Hall (York Archaeological Trust); Professor Peter Harper; Professor John Hines; Steve Howe; Dr Judith Jesch; Dr Julie Jones; Alan King; Diana Morgan; Dr J.A.F. Napier; Raghnall Ó Floinn; Professor R.I. Page; Dr Catrin Redknap; Dr Alice Roberts; Tom Sharpe; Jane Standen; Mike Stokes; Bob Trett; Dr Andrew Wawn; Sir David Wilson.

Early versions of the text have benefited considerably from comments from the following, to whom I owe many thanks: Edward Besly, Margaret Bird, Richard Brewer, Dr Nancy Edwards, John Kenyon, Dr Alan Lane, Professor James Graham-Campbell, Jeremy Knight, Professor Henry Loyn, Susan Youngs. I would also like to acknowledge the debt I owe to the historians and archaeologists on whose original research I have relied so heavily, many of whom are cited under 'Main Sources'. I am very grateful to Elin ap Hywel for editing the Welsh version of this publication, and Shanon Deal for seeking copyright permissions.

I would in particular like to thank Roger and Debbie Tebbutt, for their generous support of the Llanbedrgoch project and donation of finds to the National Museums & Galleries of Wales; Mr Archie Gillespie and Mr Peter Corbett, and all metal detectorists who have brought finds to the attention of the National Museum and allowed the Department of Archaeology & Numismatics to record them; the supervisors and site assistants at Llanbedrgoch (Jerry Bond, Evan Chapman, Mark Lewis, Mark Lodwick, Brian Milton and David Stevens) and finally, but no less importantly, to all the volunteers who have assisted on the excavation.

Quotations from primary sources in translation

The author and Museum gratefully acknowledge the following translations from medieval and later writers used in this book:

J. P. Clancy (trans.) 1970, *Armes Prydein* in *The Earliest Welsh Poetry* (London, Macmillan).

T. Conran (trans.) 1986, 'Cynddylan's Hall' in *Welsh Verse* (Bridgend, Poetry Wales Press, Seren).

G. N. Garmonsway (trans.) 1986, *The Anglo-Saxon Chronicle* (Guernsey, Everyman Classics).

C. W. Heckethorn (trans.) 1856, *The Frithjof Saga; A Scandinavian Romance*, by E. Tegner, London.

K. H. Jackson 1935, 'Stanza xxxiii', *Studies in Early Celtic Nature Poetry* (Cambridge University Press), 32.

J. Jesch 1996, 'Norse historical traditions and the Historia Gruffudd vab Kenan: Magnús berfoettr and Haraldr Hárfagri', in K. Maund, *Gruffudd ap Cynan. A Collaborative Biography* (Woodbridge, Boydell Press), 117-47.

T. Jones (trans.) 1972 (2nd edition), *Brut y Tywysogyon or Chronicle of the Princes. Red Book of Hergest Version*, Board of Celtic Studies, University of Wales History & Law Series no.16 (Cardiff, University of Wales Press).

S. Keynes & M. Lapidge (trans.) 1983, 'Aethelweard's chronicle' in *Alfred the Great. Asser's Life of King Alfred and other contemporary sources* (London, Penguin).

C. Larrington (trans.) 1996, T*he Poetic Edda* (Oxford, Oxford University Press).

H. Pálsson & P. Edwards (trans.) 1978, *Orkneyinga Saga. The History of the Earls of Orkney* (London, Chatto & Windus).

L. Thorpe (trans.) 1978, *Gerald of Wales, The Journey through Wales and Description of Wales* (London, Penguin).

A. W. Wade-Evans (trans.) 1944, *Vitae Sanctorum Britanniae et Genealogiae* (Cardiff, University of Wales Press).

D. Whitelock (trans.) 1961, *The Anglo-Saxon Chronicle, a revised translation* (London, Eyre & Spottiswoode).

D. Whitelock 1979, *English Historical Documents c. 500-1042. English Historical Documents Vol.1 (2nd edition, London).*

The excerpt from the *Annals of Ireland. Three Fragments*, translated by Professor I. Ll. Foster, is reproduced by kind permission from *Scandinavian England*, by F.T. Wainwright, edited by H.R.P. Finberg, published in 1975 by Phillimore & Co. Ltd, Shopwyke Manor Barn, Chichester, West Sussex.

Main Sources

Heathen Men (and throughout)

H.B. Clarke, M. Ní Mhaonaigh & R. Ó Floinn (eds) 1998, *Ireland and Scandinavia in the Early Viking Age*, Dublin.

W. Davies 1982, *Wales in the Early Middle Ages. Studies in the Early History of Britain*, Leicester.

W. Davies 1990, *Patterns of Power in Early Wales*, Oxford.

P. Foote & D. M. Wilson 1970, *The Viking Achievement,* London.

J. Graham-Campbell, with C. Batey, H. Clarke, R. I. Page & N. S. Price 1994, *Cultural Atlas of the Viking World,* Abingdon.

J. Graham-Campbell & C.E. Batey 1998, *Vikings in Scotland. An Archaeological Survey,* Edinburgh.

J. Haywood 1995, *The Penguin Historical Atlas of the Vikings,* Harmondsworth.

H. R. Loyn 1976, *The Vikings in Wales,* Dorothea Coke, Memorial Lecture, London.

H. R. Loyn 1994, *The Viking Age in Britain*. Historical Association Studies, Oxford.

E. Roesdahl & D.M. Wilson (eds) 1992, *From Viking to Crusader: The Scandinavians and Europe 800-1200* (Copenhagen/New York: Nordic Council of Ministers, 22nd Council of Europe Exhibition).

P. Sawyer (ed.) 1997, *The Oxford Illustrated History of the Vikings*, Oxford.

A. P. Smyth 1975, *Scandinavian York and Dublin*, Dublin (2 vols.).

Birth of a Viking Myth

N. F. Blake (ed.) 1962, *The Saga of the Jomsvikings*, London.

A. G. Moffat 1903, 'Palnatoki in Wales', *Saga Book of the Viking Club* 3/2, 163-73.

E. Peters 1991, *The Summer of the Danes*, London.

G. E. Powell & Eiríkur Magnússon (trans.) 1864, *Icelandic legends* (collected by Jón Arnasson), London.

G. E. Powell & Eiríkur Magnússon (trans.) 1866, *Icelandic legends* (collected by Jón Arnasson). Second Series London.

A. Waun 1992, 'The spirit of 1892: sagas, saga-steads and Victorian philology', *Saga-Book of the Viking Club* 23, 213-52.

R. Williams 1990, *People of the Black Mountains II. The Eggs and the Eagle*. London, Chatto & Windus.

Charting New Waters

Anon 1846, 'Saxon coins found at Bangor, Caernarvonshire', *Archaeologia Cambrensis* l, 276.

J. O'Donovan (ed.) 1860, *Annals of Ireland. Three Fragments by Dubhaltach mac Firbisigh*, Dublin.

R. Fenton 1811, *A Historical Tour through Pembrokeshire*, London, esp. 135-36, 161, 412, 538, 555.

W. B. Jones 1875, 'Inaugural Address, Carmarthen Meeting', *Archaeologia Cambrensis* 6, 388 ff.

N. Nicolaysen 1882, *Langskibet fra Gokstad ved Sandefjord (The Viking Ship Discovered at Gokstad in Norway)*. Kristiana.

D. Powel 1584, *The historie of Cambria, now called Wales: A part of the most famous Yland of Brytaine, Written in the British language above two hundreth yeares past:* [Caradoc of Llancarfan, 1156]: *translated into English by H. Lluyd, Gentleman: Converted, augmented and continued out of records and best approoved Authors, by David Powe*l, London.

Viking Place-names

B. G. Charles 1934, *Old Norse Relations with Wales*, University of Wales Press, Cardiff.

B. G. Charles 1938, *Non-Celtic Place-Names in Wales*, London.

B. G. Charles 1992, *Pembrokeshire Place-names*, National Library of Wales (2 vols, Aberystwyth).

G. Fellows-Jensen 1992, 'Scandinavian place-names of the Irish Sea province', in J. Graham-Campbell (ed.), *Viking Treasure from the North West. The Cuerdale Hoard and its Context*, National Museums & Galleries of Merseyside Occasional Papers Liverpool Museum No.5, 31-42.

G. O. Pierce 1984, 'The evidence of place-names', Appendix II to *Glamorgan County History* Volume II (ed. G. Williams), Cardiff, 456-92.

D. R. Paterson 1921, 'Early Cardiff. With a short account of its street-names and surrounding place-names', *Transactions of the Cardiff Naturalists' Society* 54, 11-71.

M. Richards 1962, 'Norse Place-names in Wales', in B. Ó Cuív (ed.), *Proceedings of the First International Congress of Celtic Studies, Dublin, 6-10 July, 1959*, Dublin, 51-60; reprinted in B.Ó Cuív 1975, *The Impact of the Scandinavian Invasions on the Celtic-speaking Peoples c.800-1100AD*, Dublin.

Viking Blood

I. Morgan-Watkins 1952, 'Blood groups in Wales and the Marches', *Man* (1952), 83-86.

I. Morgan-Watkins 1986, 'ABO blood group distribution in Wales in relation to human settlement', in P. S. Sawyer & E. Sunderland (eds), *Genetic & Population Studies in Wales*, University of Wales Press, Cardiff.

W. T. W. Potts 1976, 'History and blood groups in the British Isles', in P. H. Sawyer (ed.), *Medieval Settlement*, 236-53.

E. Sunderland 1976, 'Comment on 'History and blood groups in the British Isles' by W. T. W. Potts', in P. H. Sawyer (ed.), *Medieval Settlement*, 254-61.

The Native Kingdoms

W. Davies 1982, *Wales in the Early Middle Ages*. Studies in the Early History of Britain, Leicester.

W. Rees 1951, *An Historical Atlas of Wales from Early to Modern Times*, Cardiff.

The First Coming

J. Graham-Campbell 1995, 'The Irish Sea Vikings; raiders and settlers', in T. Scott & P. Starkey (eds), *The Middle Ages in the North West*, 59-83.

S. Keynes & M. Lapidge 1983, *Alfred the Great. Asser's Life of King Alfred and other contemporary sources*, London.

The Battle of Buttington

W. Boyd Dawkins 1873, 'On some human remains found at Buttington, Montgomeryshire', *Montgomeryshire Collections* 6, 141-45.
C.W. Dymond 1900, 'On the identification of the site of "Buttingtune" of the *Saxon Chronicle*, anno 894', *Montgomeryshire Collections* 31, 337-46.
T. Morgan Owen 1874, 'The battle of Buttington 894 with a brief sketch of the affairs of Powys and Mercia', *Montgomeryshire Collections* 7, 249-66.
I. McDougall 1995, 'Discretion and deceit: a re-examination of military stratagem in *Egils saga*', in T. Scott & P. Starkey (eds), *The Middle Ages in the North-West*, Oxford, 109-42.

A Siege at Chester

F. T. Wainwright 1942, 'North-west Mercia, 871-924', *Transactions of the Historical Society of Lancashire and Cheshire* 94, 3-56.
S. Ward & others 1994, *Excavations at Chester. Saxon Occupation within the Roman Fortress. Sites excavated 1971-81*. Archaeological Service Excavation and Survey Reports No.7, Chester.

The Second Phase

D. Griffiths 1995, 'The north-west Mercian burhs. A reappraisal', *Anglo-Saxon Studies in Archaeology & History* 8, 75-86.
H. Quinnel, M. R. Blockley & P. Berridge 1994, *Excavations at Rhuddlan, Clwyd 1969-73. Mesolithic to Medieval*, CBA Research Report 95.

Öngul's Isle

F. T. Wainwright 1948, 'Ingimund's invasion', *English Historical Review* 63, 145-69.

The Later Raids

J. Jesch 1996, 'Norse historical traditions and the *Historia Gruffud vab Kenan*: Magnús berfoettr and Haraldr hárfagri', in K. Maund, *Gruffudd ap Cynan. A Collaborative Biography*, 117-47.
D. Longley 1991, 'The excavation of Castell, Porth Trefadog, a coastal promontory fort in North Wales', *Medieval Archaeology* 35, 64-85.
D. Simon Evans 1990, *Historia Gruffud vab Kenan*, Lampeter.

The Viking Warrior

M. Biddle & B. Kjølbye-Biddle 1992, 'Repton and the Vikings', *Antiquity* 66, 36-51.
J. K. Knight 1996, 'Late Roman and Post-Roman Caerwent. Some evidence from the metalwork', *Archaeologia Cambrensis* 145, 34-66.

M. Redknap 1992, 'Remarkable Viking find in remote site', *Amgueddfa* (Winter 1992), 9.
W. A. Seaby & P. Woodfield 1980, 'Viking stirrups from England and their background', *Medieval Archaeology* 24, 87-122.

Masters of Wide Seas

G. Bersu & D. M. Wilson 1966, *Three Viking Graves in the Isle of Man*, Society of Medieval Archaeology Monograph 1, London.
O. Crumlin-Pedersen 1991, 'Ship types and sizes AD 800-1400', in O. Crumlin-Pedersen (ed.), *Aspects of Maritime Scandinavia AD 200-1200*, Roskilde, 69-82.
A. G. Moffat 1901-3, 'Palnatoki in Wales', *Saga-Book of the Viking Club 3*, 163-73.
O. Morgan 1878, 'The ancient Danish vessel, found near the mouth of the River Usk', *Archaeological Journal* 35, 403-5.
O. Morgan 1882, *Ancient Danish vessel discovered at the mouth of the Usk*, Monmouthshire and Caerleon Antiquarian Association, Newport, 23-26.

Traders

G. C. Boon, 1986, *Welsh Coin Hoards*, Cardiff.
D. W. Dykes, 1976 *Anglo-Saxon Coins in the National Museum of Wales*, Cardiff.
D. Griffiths 1992, 'The coastal trading ports of the Irish Sea', in J. Graham-Campbell (ed.), *Viking Treasure from the North West. The Cuerdale Hoard and its Context*, National Museums & Galleries of Merseyside Occasional Papers Liverpool Museum No. 5, 63-72.
J. A. A. Rutter 1985, 'The pottery' in D. J. Mason, *Excavations at Chester. 26-42 Lower Bridge Street 1974-6. The Dark Age and Saxon Periods*, Grosvenor Museum Archaeological Excavation and Survey Report No.3, 40-56.

Breaking New Ground. Llanbedrgoch: from Farm to Trading Centre

Archaeology in Wales. CBA Wales Journal, reports therein.
M. Redknap 1998, 'The quest for Anglesey Vikings - the evidence of coin hoards and archaeology', *Minerva* 9.4, 49-51.
M. Redknap 1998, 'Limits of Viking influence in Wales', *British Archaeology* 40, 12-13.
M. Redknap 1999, 'Excavation of a Viking Age site at Llanbedrgoch on Anglesey', *Viking Heritage Newsletter* 4, 9-11.
For further information, see *Digging for Vikings* on *http://www.nmgw.ac.uk/archaeol/anglesey/*

House and Home

P. F. Wallace 1992, *The Viking Age Buildings of Dublin*, National Museum of Ireland Medieval Dublin Excavations 1962-81, Series A, vol. l, Royal Irish Academy.

Dress

T. Fanning 1994, *Viking Age Ringed Pins from Dublin*, National Museum of Ireland Medieval Dublin Excavations 1962-81, Series B. vol. 4, Royal Irish Academy.

Craft Processes

J. Graham-Campbell, with C. Batey, H. Clarke, R. I. Page & N. S. Price 1994, *Cultural Atlas of the Viking World*, Abingdon.

Viking Ornamental Style

R. N. Bailey 1980, *Viking Age Sculpture in Northern England*, London.
N. Edwards 1999, 'Viking-influenced sculpture in North Wales; its ornament and context', *Church Archaeology* 3, 5-16.
J. Graham-Campell 1985, 'Two Scandinavian disc broches of Viking Age date from England', *Medieval Archaeology* 65, 448-49.
S. Margeson 1984-6, 'A group of late Saxon mounts from Norfolk', *Norfolk Archaeology* 39, 323-27.
O. Owen & R. Trett 1979/80, 'A Viking Urnes style mount from Sedgeford', *Norfolk Archaeology* 37, 353-54. & 'Further Note' by S. M. Margeson, 355.
D. M. Wilson & O. Klindt-Jensen 1966, *Viking Art*, London.
D. M. Wilson 1995, 'Scandinavian ornamental influence in the Irish Sea region in the Viking Age', in T. Scott & P. Starkey (eds), *The Middle Ages in the North West*, 36-57.

Pagan Viking Belief

R. I. Page 1990, *Norse Myths*, London.
E. Roesdahl & D. M. Wilson (eds) 1992, *From Viking to Crusader: The Scandinavians and Europe 800-1200* (Copenhagen/New York; Nordic Council of Ministers, 22nd Council of Europe Exhibition).

Death and Burial

N. Edwards 1985, 'A possible Viking grave from Benllech, Anglesey', *Anglesey Antiquarian Society and Field Club Transactions* (1985), 19-24.
C. Fox 1940, 'An Irish bronze pin from Anglesey', *Archaeologia Cambrensis* 95, 248.
D. Freke *et al* (forthcoming), *Excavations on St Patrick's Isle, Peel, Isle of Man: Prehistoric, Viking, Medieval and Later, 1982-8* (Liverpool University Press).
R. Ó Floinn 1998,'The archaeology of the Early Viking Age in Ireland', in H. B. Clarke, M. Ní Mhaonaigh & R. Ó Floinn (eds), *Ireland and Scandinavia in the Early Viking Age*, Dublin, 131-65.
F. G. Smith 1931-2, 'Talacre and the Viking grave', *Proceedings of the Llandudno, Colwyn Bay and District Field Club* 17, 42-50.

I. Williams 1945, 'Recent finds in Anglesey: Benllech', *Anglesey Antiquarian Society and Field Club Transactions* (1945), 21-23

Vikings as Christians. The End in Wales

N. J. Higham 1997, *The Death of Anglo-Saxon England*, Sutton Press, Stroud.

M. K. Lawson 1993, *Cnut: the Danes in England in the early eleventh century*, London and New York.

R. Moon 1978, 'Viking runic inscriptions in Wales', *Archaeologia Cambrensis* 127, 124-26.

V. E. Nash-Williams, 1950 *The Early Christian Monuments of Wales*, Cardiff.

R. I. Page 1973, *An Introduction to English Runes*, London.

R. I. Page 1998, *Runes and Runic Inscriptions. Collected Essays on Anglo-Saxon and Viking Runes*, Boydell Press.